CW01082630

*A great adventure, combining history and exploration.
It will inspire you to get out there.*
Dan Snow, Historian & Broadcaster

Historical, tragical and comical.
Andy Martin, Author

*An enchanting tale, full of curiosities and just the
sort of telling detail that I enjoy. This is a delight.
A sensitive, modern and yet strangely timeless odyssey
through the harsh Berber lands of rock and dust.*
Benedict Allen, Explorer, Author & Broadcaster

RETURN TO THE

Berber Village

Paul Olding (signature)

Paul Olding

The Book Guild Ltd

First published in Great Britain in 2022 by
The Book Guild Ltd
Unit E2, Airfield Business Park
Harrison Road
Market Harborough
Leicestershire, LE16 7UL
Freephone: 0800 999 2982
www.bookguild.co.uk
Email: info@bookguild.co.uk
Twitter: @bookguild

Typeset in 11pt Minion Pro

Printed and bound in the UK by TJ Books LTD, Padstow, Cornwall

ISBN 978 1914471 094

British Library Cataloguing in Publication Data.
A catalogue record for this book is available from the British Library.

To my father Frank Olding, who loved to travel.

Contents

Preface   ix

1. The Book in the Attic   1
2. Oxford   10
3. Lord of the Atlas   22
4. Planning   26
5. In Their Footsteps   35
6. Travelling through Morocco   40
7. Arrival in Marrakech   47
8. Journey into the Mountains   60
9. The Berber Village   74
10. At Home in the Village   85
11. A Run-in with the Authorities   98
12. Life in the Berber Village   105
13. A Chance Encounter   120
14. Au Revoir   128
15. Time Travel at Telouet   136
16. Discovery at Ouarzazate   145
17. Gorges and Campervans   154
18. Potters near the Dunes   160
19. Hollywood of the Sahara   166

20: Return (Again) to the Berber Village   170
21. A Warm Welcome   174
22. Celebrating Eid   183
23. Final Farewell   189
24. Back Home   195

Epilogue   205

Acknowledgements   209

Preface

1955 was an interesting year. It was the year that Albert Einstein died aged seventy-six. It was also the year that Winston Churchill resigned as Prime Minister of Great Britain, citing declining health. It was the year Jim Henson created Kermit the Frog, Walt Disney opened Disneyland in California and the USA launched the USS Nautilus, the world's first nuclear-powered submarine. It was also the year that five Oxford University students purchased a rather battered ex-army truck, and under the banner of the auspicious Oxford University Exploration Club, set off on an expedition to the High Atlas Mountains of southern Morocco. Their plan was to find a Berber village effectively isolated from the outside world, to explore how the village was organised and managed, see what crops they grew and how they grew them, to uncover any unique local crafts and to conduct a biological study of the animals and plants of the region. Some years later, while I too was studying for a degree at Oxford, I stumbled upon their story.

The leader of the expedition was a zoologist called Bryan Clarke and he'd written a book about the trip entitled *Berber Village*. In it, Bryan gave a vivid account of adventure and derring-do as the five students set off to a country in a state of political upheaval, perched as it was on the precipice of change. It was also a time when the powerful and charismatic Pasha of Marrakech, T'hami el Glaoui, still maintained effective rule over much of southern Morocco. The team even had direct contact with the Glaoui family, who provided the students with letters of invitation and assorted hospitality in their rich and exotic kasbahs. But little did they know that Morocco was on the brink of independence from French control. El Glaoui was a French sympathiser and supporter and had made his considerable fortune in exploiting this relationship, but in ultimately backing the wrong horse, he and his entire family would not survive the transition to the new independent state. Through the students' personal diaries, notes and photographs, the team had inadvertently recorded at first hand, not just a snapshot of life in a Berber village, but also a unique moment in time just before the fall of the French regime, the fall of el Glaoui and the rise of modern independent Morocco.

It was while reading the wonderfully thick, heavyset pages of Bryan's book, the scent of which alone transported me back in time, that I had the idea to try and retrace the footsteps of this expedition, to locate and return to their Berber village and see how life had changed since the students set up camp there, underneath a walnut tree.

Having tracked down a number of the original team members, each said they had very fond memories of their youthful Moroccan expedition and agreed for me to meet and interview them. By their own admission, back in 1955, the students were quite naive of the escalating political situation in Morocco. Each was generous in sharing with me a bounty of photographs and documents and gave great personal insight into their time on the trip, the people they'd met and the changing political landscape they had witnessed, sometimes at very close quarters.

I thought it would be useful (and fun) to have some company on my journey of discovery and convinced my young nephew, James, to come with me. We sourced a local travel outfit who admitted that, while they'd never heard of the Berber village we hoped to visit, they would do their best to get us up into the mountains and try and find it. In March 2007, we set off to see what we could discover. Having returned in one piece (albeit bearing a considerable odour according to James's then girlfriend, now wife, who picked us up from the airport), James and I returned again in November 2009, and this time (unknown to us until I happened to read it on the plane going over) we arrived during the Muslim celebration of Eid al-Adha. For both trips, all we had to help us navigate our route, both physically and socially, was Bryan's book, a hand-drawn map showing the village's rough location in the mountains and some old photographs generously provided by the original members.

This is the story of the original 1955 expedition, their adventures across Morocco during a time of political change and nationalistic bloodshed, the village and villagers they studied hidden away in a valley in the High Atlas Mountains and how, just over fifty years later, I followed in their footsteps and returned to the Berber Village.

1

The Book in the Attic

My family home had an attic stuffed full of memories, both mine and my parents'. Access was via a stepladder brought in from the garden shed and set up on the narrow second-storey landing. There wasn't much room and, when erected, one leg of the ladder was precariously close to the top of the stairs. Once you climbed up and removed a wooden panel in the ceiling, you pulled yourself through the hole into the dark, dusty loft above. The loft would later be converted into a more useable and cleaner storage space, boasting electric lighting and one of those integrated folding ladders with a handrail which now provides a more leisurely mode of entrance. But back then, having heaved yourself into the dark abyss, you'd call out and someone below would pass up one of those old loft lights (where the naked bulb was surrounded by a protective cage) and, hooking it over a nail protruding from one of the wooden cross-beams, you'd gingerly walk over the poorly illuminated sections of hardboard laid across the joists so you didn't fall through the ceiling below. Everything up there was covered in a layer of dust, which at that time included old skis and ski boots, some barely used dumbbells and other free weights, our old record player (I'm unsure why we kept it as it no longer worked) and some old toys I couldn't get rid of, including a set of original Star Wars figures from the early 1980s, which would eventually be passed on to my sons. There was my dad's darkroom enlarger (unused since before I was born and now boxed up), plus his old 78s record collection, including some real gems from the 1950s, such as 'Rock around the Clock' by Mr Bill Hailey and his Comets and 'Earth Angel' by the Crew-Cuts, records which only recently I was able to play aloud having finally sourced a player that could play 78s. There were also a few glass tanks and vivaria that had housed various exotic pets when I was younger, plus drawings I'd made in primary school, boxes of my exercise books and folders from my GCSEs and A-levels, my badge collection, my key ring collection and my beer mat collection. OK, so I'm a bit of a hoarder.

One rainy afternoon while I was home from university for the holidays, I had taken myself up into the loft to have a poke about. With so many *treasures*, it was always fun to see what I could find, often for no better reason than to know it was still there and hadn't been thrown away or sold. Tucked away in a corner of the loft was a box of old books. I remember when I was younger, these books used to reside in an old walnut bookcase located in our spare room, but when that room became an office, the bookshelf was commandeered for more relevant (and recent) publications, and the books were sent up to the attic. These books belonged to my mother who, when quizzed, recalled that back in the 1950s, she'd subscribed to something called the 'Travel Book Club' (based in Charing Cross Road, London) and had purchased a number of their hardbacks, all priced around eighteen shillings. Glancing across their pastel-coloured spines revealed enchanting titles,

such as *Desert Taxi*, about an English couple who drove across
the Sahara from Algiers to Kano in Nigeria in a twenty-year-
old Austin London taxi. There was also *Two-Up: By Scooter
to Australia* where, three years later, the *same* couple made
an even more impressive journey, driving from London to
Australia on a moped!

In amongst the books, I happened across one title that,
unknown to me at that moment, would set me on a path of
adventure and discovery. It was entitled *Berber Village – The Story
of the Oxford University Expedition to the High Atlas Mountains
of Morocco*. The cover jacket featured a rather enigmatic, almost
monochrome (beige with light beige) image of three Berbers
dressed in dark cloaks and white turbans, sat with their mule,
gazing out across a wide mountain valley to a village nestled
into the slope opposite. Blowing off the dust, I reached for the
loft light and opened the book. The blurb on the inside sleeve
instantly piqued my curiosity:

> In the summer of 1955, five undergraduates officially
> sponsored by the Oxford University Exploration Club,
> set off in a truck they named Tartarin to visit the Berber
> tribes in the Atlas Mountains of southern Morocco. The
> party included a zoologist, a botanist and an ethnologist,
> and their aim was to study the people and fauna and
> flora of this remote part of North Africa. This is a light
> hearted account of the expedition by its leader, who
> has the rare ability to tell a good story with grace and
> humour.

Berber Village by Bryan Clarke ©Bryan Clarke 1959

The book was written by a man called Bryan Clarke who, back in 1955, was noted as being a zoology student studying at Magdalen College in Oxford. He was joined on the trip by four other students: Humphrey Beckett who was reading History at Worcester College, noted as the expedition's 'ethnologist', plus geographer Peter Galloway, botanist John Newbould and a second zoologist called Colin Pennycuick, all studying at Merton College. They were also briefly joined by a postgraduate student called Charles Pasternak (Magdalen) who was down as being a biochemist.

As an Oxford undergraduate myself, at that time in my first year studying biology at Jesus College, I had invertedly stumbled across a story written by and about my academic forebears.

From the outset, I felt I had a deep connection with these men despite the many years separating my time from theirs in the 'City of Dreaming Spires'.

Diving into chapter one, Bryan was straight in on the action. He recounted a moment in wonderfully vivid detail from early on in the expedition, when the group were driving down through northern Morocco. Events were unfolding before them that threatened to end the expedition long before they got anywhere near the Atlas Mountains and the Berber village of which the book took its title. The team had just crossed by ferry from Gibraltar into Morocco and their truck had broken down. Now stuck in the middle of nowhere, no one would stop to offer help or even give them a lift to a garage to source repairs. The hapless students were finally accosted by a Frenchman in uniform with a submachine gun, who'd heard news on the wireless of 'terrorist attacks', hence the reason perhaps no one was willing to stop to help. He said there'd been reports of bombs going off in nearby Casablanca. Sometime later, one of the students finally caught a lift, sat in the back of an ambulance carrying wounded civilians to hospital.

I was hooked. This was a Morocco I didn't recognise and had never heard about. This was a country ripping itself apart as the colonial French administrators (and their native Moroccan allies) were in the process of being ousted, to be replaced by a new, nationalistic regime (Moroccan independence took place a year later in the Spring of 1956). Through no inherent planning of their own, the university students had found themselves in a country at a pivotal moment of divisive change. I soon realised Bryan Clarke's book, found by chance in my parents' attic, was more than just an account of a summer jaunt by a group of university students. This book gave a detailed snapshot, an eyewitness account even, of a moment just before the modern independent country of Morocco came into being. Through the places they visited, the people they met, the sights and sounds they encountered, Bryan had managed to chronicle the final dying days of the French administration (or possibly, more accurately, French *occupation*) of the country.

I had been to Morocco once before, with the travel company Exodus back in 1990, during the summer vacation of what was my lower sixth year (year twelve in new money), between GCSEs and A-levels. At that time, Exodus was a bit of a new breed of tour operator, offering something they called 'Adventure Travel'. This was advertised as sitting in the back of a truck, driving across the dusty desert, camping in the wilds, climbing mountains and roughing it sort of thing. We travelled all over Morocco and into the High Atlas, climbing Djebel Toubkal, the highest mountain in North Africa. On that trip, I'd explored many of Morocco's finest cities, from the stinking tanneries of Fes, to the souks of Meknes, to the eye-watering chaos of Marrakech (staying at the wonderfully named Hotel Fuh-call). I'd traded with Berbers, was caught in a sandstorm, got lost climbing a gorge and even saw the famous Moroccan goats climbing in trees. I'd seen quite a good stretch of modern, bustling, independent Morocco. But the members of the 1955 expedition would have seen and experienced a completely different country, one that was still (but only just) under the control of the French.

Inspired by Bryan's book, I wondered if I could revisit some of the places he had written about decades earlier and see how things had changed or indeed, remained the same? I was interested to discover whether life, particularly for the Berbers, had altered in any way with Moroccan independence. Might it be possible to track down some of the people the students had met on their journey and see how they or their descendants were faring? Most of all, would it be possible to retrace the students' footsteps and return to their Berber village?

My first plan of action was to see if I could locate and make contact with Bryan, the expedition leader, hoping that he was still alive. When I first came across Bryan's book, it was the early 1990s, long before the internet properly kicked in, and so all I had to go on was the knowledge he'd studied at Magdalen College in Oxford. I wrote Bryan a letter introducing myself and my wish to follow in the footsteps of his Moroccan expedition and sent it to his college on the off chance they had a forwarding address. But this is where things get a bit hazy. I don't recall ever getting a reply, but my own life at that time was overtaken by a number of life-changing events.

While studying for my degree in biology, my father (to whom this book is dedicated) passed away, losing his battle to cancer. A year later, I had my final exams. Then, I decided to stay on at Oxford to continue my studies, embarking on a doctorate in animal behaviour under the guidance of the eminent zoologist Prof Marian Stamp Dawkins. The focus of my research centred on the vocalisations of a group of species of tree frogs parping away in the Wet Tropics region of Australia. Back then, frogs didn't get much attention as far as academic research was concerned. They were seen as academically uninteresting compared to the 'Furries and the Pretties' as one academic put it, to which she was referring to mammals, birds and butterflies, not the current meaning of 'Furries', which I believe describes people who dress up in animal costumes. But ever since my youth, when I built a wildlife pond in the garden of our house in south-east London, I quite liked frogs. Three wet seasons later and I managed to pass my doctorate, but with academia now losing its grip on my continued attention, I decided it was time to leave Oxford and try and get a job.

For years, I'd been interested in making wildlife television shows and had grand ambitions to be the next David Attenborough or the next Chris Packham (I'd applied to be a presenter on the *Really Wild Show* several times). Over the years, I'd written to countless people at the BBC and received many polite rejections, but finally landed a junior role (Acting Trainee Junior Researcher) on the weekly magazine science show *Tomorrow's World*, based out of White City in London. With that, and then marriage to my high school sweetheart, my plan to return to Morocco to try and find Bryan's Berber village was all but forgotten. But then, in 2005, while still in the employ of the BBC Science department, I once again came across Bryan's book, now located on my own bookshelf. More than a decade had passed since I first read about Bryan's adventures, and it was now fifty years since the university students had set out on their trip. Reinvigorated by what was a 'Golden Jubilee' 50th anniversary, I once again set about trying to track down the six members of the expedition. Now with the aid of a much-advanced World Wide Web, I had far greater success.

Expedition leader Bryan Campbell Clarke popped up in my search engine as an Emeritus Professor at Nottingham University. He'd become a world-renowned zoologist who, having left Oxford, went on to have an illustrious career in animal genetics.

Along with Bryan, I managed to get in touch with Humphrey Beckett. Although Humphrey had been studying history at Worcester, once he'd completed his degree, he went on to study medicine and become a psychiatrist and had since retired to southern France.

One name from the list of expedition team members that stuck out for me was Colin Pennycuick. While I was studying at Oxford, Colin's work on bird flight was considered essential reading in our tutorials on vertebrate anatomy – I located him still actively studying the mechanics of animal flight at the University of Bristol.

The other two team members were geographer Peter

Galloway and botanist John Newbould, but sadly my internet searches for these two gentlemen came up short. Merton College confirmed both had completed their degrees but had no knowledge of their current whereabouts.

The sixth member of the expedition was Charles Pasternak, who would join the group just for a couple of weeks. Charles had forged a distinguished career in biochemistry. That name 'Pasternak' also sounded familiar – when I met him in London, he revealed that Boris Pasternak, author of *Dr Zhivago*, was his uncle.

I arranged to interview the four members I'd managed to track down and each were very generous in giving up their time in reminiscing about their 1955 Moroccan adventure. All four also provided numerous photographs, journals and documents which helped me build a first-hand picture of what life was like in Morocco at that time, not just for the visiting students, but for the Berber people and the village they studied, plus the wider country as a whole, still under the control of the French. They also granted me permission to quote from their interviews and their diaries when writing this book, and to use their photographs, without which, as you will discover, my attempt to follow in the students' footsteps and, moreover, to connect with the past, would have amounted to nothing. Armed with a growing folder of research materials and resources, I could now start to plan my own expedition.

2

Oxford

The idea of mounting a summer expedition to Morocco (as opposed to elsewhere) happened pretty much by chance and came to Bryan during a tutorial session in 1954. Oxford University back then, and indeed when I was there, worked slightly differently to other universities. There were lectures to attend and, for the sciences, practical classes (known as *demonstrations*) to muddle through, but most of the learning actually happened through the ages-old tutorial system. This generally involved writing a weekly essay (or equivalent) set by your tutor, whereby you were sent off with a title and a reading list to research a topic and then explore a specific question in essay form. At one particular tutorial, by Bryan's own admission he had written a particularly bad essay and his tutor was keen to change the subject. He asked what Bryan had planned for the following year's summer holiday. Bryan noted that:

I had no idea, but I appreciated the diversion. Anything was better than discussing the essay, so I mentioned

Morocco... I can't give any respectable reason but the name was connected in our minds with romance and the Mysterious East.

It turned out that Bryan's tutor was very interested in Morocco and, with the dire tutorial essay now forgotten, he eagerly suggested that a study of its wildlife would be 'very instructive', as little work had been done on the subject. His tutor explained that during the last Ice Age, many European animals had been forced into Spain and across into Morocco, as the ice sheets formed a land bridge into North Africa. But then, as the world warmed up and the ice retreated, many of the animals that had evolved in cooler climates headed up the mountains and had been isolated there ever since. Bryan recalled that his tutor continued:

It would be rewarding to find out the effects of this long period of isolation, during which the populations must have changed and become adapted to the conditions of their new home.

Enthused by his tutor's interest, Bryan started to ponder how he could organise a trip to go and collect these animals – now trapped, as it were, on the upper slopes of the cooler mountains surrounded by hot desert plateaus – and bring them back to Oxford for further study.

Life at Oxford University in 1955 was slightly different to when I went there in the 1990s. Admittedly, a great deal was unchanged and had remained the same for centuries, such as the costumes, the archaic traditions and the terminology, but speaking to the original expedition members, I discovered that their lives involved far more *shenanigans* (for want of a better word) than I'd experienced while I was there. With most young men at the time having been shipped off to do their National

Service prior to coming up to Oxford, on arrival at the university, the students prided themselves on being worldly wise, but they still liked being looked after. For Bryan, the college staff, or 'Scouts' as they were called, acted as key personnel in pastoral care. When I spoke to him, he recalled:

> Bryan: "There were the college Scouts who came in the morning bringing you hot water, enough to shave in and one of those old Victorian bowls with the steaming hot jug. He laid my fire in my sitting room and lit it for me and I think he probably cleaned my shoes as well. He also educated me, because they had very firm ideas about how young gentlemen should behave and if you didn't behave in the correct manner, the Scouts made their disapproval very clear. However, it was perfectly permissible for you to have young ladies in your rooms if you passed enough financial reward to the Scout and so on, and that was made use of on occasion…"

There seemed to be a lot of clandestine activities going on in the 1950s, particularly involving young women, who were not allowed into the all-male colleges. Charles Pasternak also shared some furtive memories:

> Charles: "I remember a friend of mine actually smuggled a girl in one day and she spent the night with him at college and in the morning, he put her into a hamper. I remember helping him carry this hamper out through the lodge in front of all the Porters."

In my time, there were no fires to be lit (we had central heating), and if I wanted a shave, I knew where the bathrooms were. With the advent of co-educational colleges, there was never a curfew for 'young ladies' staying over, though the single beds in our college rooms were extraordinarily narrow, perhaps to act as a discouragement. From what I learnt from the expedition team, Oxford in the 1950s sounded like a rather boisterous place.

> Bryan: "Everybody knew who you were and when you went in for breakfast, they'd tick your name off and they wouldn't have to ask it. And when they knew unruly behaviour was going to happen, they would put out in conspicuous places all their old furniture and stuff they didn't want, knowing that the drunken young students would come and put it on a bonfire and then because they knew everybody's name, they just wrote down 'one armchair – Joe Bloggs' and then Joe Bloggs got the bill. This way they kept their furniture up to date with new replacements."

Curfews at that time were strict, and if you weren't back in college when the doors were locked, you had to find ways to get back to your bedroom.

> Charles: "I remember tearing a pair of trousers climbing into Magdalen. For some reason the Dons had left a ladder on the inside of the wall. This was useful to help you climb down without hurting yourself. But to get up onto the wall in the first place, you had to haul yourself up along a lamppost and the lamppost had spikes pointing down on them which were useful to grasp and haul yourself up, but if you weren't careful the spike would go up into your trousers…"

Alongside these high jinks, there were still lectures and tutorials to attend, essays to write and, invariably, an eclectic social life to lead. For Bryan, now there was also the task of trying to come up with potential research ideas that he could shape into a summer expedition to Morocco. Driven on by his tutor, Bryan started to put together a proposal, but for any university expedition to go ahead, he would have to get it approved by the senior committee members of the famous Oxford University Exploration Club.

Three decades or so after Bryan, in September 1991, I went up to Oxford University. I never discovered why one goes 'up' to Oxford (and conversely comes back 'down' when one has finished their studies and leaves the University), but then again, I soon discovered Oxford (like so many old institutions) was full of its own very weird and quaint terminology. I would later row for my college in *Torpids*, wear *Sub-Fusc* (dinner suit, gown, white tie and mortar board) for my exams and would often arrive prior to the start of term in *minus one week*. I had won a place to study biology at Jesus College located in Turl Street in the very heart of the city and immediately dived into both college and university life (the two run concomitantly but can play out very differently), joining assorted societies and clubs. One such organisation was the Oxford University Exploration Club or OUEC for short.

Just as it was in Bryan's time, the OUEC was a rather hallowed and venerated institution, boasting many famous explorers from its illustrious alumni. It included people who had made the first ascents of such-and-such mountain or made the first crossings of this-and-that desert. Many past members had gone on to lead even greater expeditions or rise through the ranks of institutions like the Foreign Office and become ambassadors. As well as attending weekly illustrated talks given by eminent explorers, OUEC members were also actively encouraged to organise their own summer expeditions. Just like Bryan's 1955 Moroccan adventure, an expedition was generally centred around a biological or geological survey in some far-flung place.

To gain official Oxford University backing for your expedition, you had to write up a detailed proposal, including a budget and a plan of logistics, and for biological surveys, a detailed methodology. You would then submit your proposal to the Expedition Council for approval. While the day-to-day running of the club was overseen by university students (of which later I would become the OUEC Treasurer), the Expedition Council was made up of a committee of Oxford Dons, mostly elderly men and women drawn from the departments of biology and geography. Some of these were quite formidable characters who could singularly rip apart an ill-thought-out expedition proposal without breaking a sweat.

Just as they'd done for decades, when I was at Oxford, the Expedition Council would go through the submissions with a fine-tooth comb and on first reading, invariably send them back for the nascent teams to address their 'feedback'. If you hoped to stand any chance of success, you would do what was required, then resubmit your proposal to the committee and hope they then approved your expedition.

For my own part, I was an active member of the OUEC and organised two university approved expeditions, the first in 1993, grandly titled 'The Oxford University Expedition to North Australia'. This was a summer spent counting and studying cane toads (large, poisonous amphibians that could easily grow to twice the size of your hand). Having been introduced to Australia from Hawaii in 1935 in the hope they'd control the ravenous cane beetles feasting on the cane crops across Queensland, the cane toad population had exploded and with it came all manner of side effects, such as the poisoning of livestock along with the endemic wildlife, all on account of the cane toad's highly potent natural toxicity. We studied and compared the toad populations around Townsville (where they had been first introduced) and the ominously named Hell's Gate Roadhouse out near the border with the Northern Territory where the toads had recently invaded.

My second expedition proved much harder to get past the Expedition Council and was called 'The Oxford University Scuba Diving Expedition to Barbados' or 'Barbados Scuba Dive '95' for short. The learned committee had a good chuckle when I first submitted my proposal, accusing me of trying to gain University funds for a fun little diving holiday. But I'd done my homework – I'd teamed up with a diving organisation in Barbados who were worried about unqualified divers causing irreparable damage to the marine environment around the island. Together, we came up with a plan to survey the popular dive sites of Carlisle Bay, just outside the capital Bridgetown. The end goal was to use our data to convince the Bajan government to implement an underwater nature reserve which would then impose limits on the daily numbers of divers. And would you believe it, it worked and our study area was subsequently designated a protected marine area.

With OUEC backing, not only were you awarded a small sum of money from the University to help towards funding your trip, but you now had a bit of clout behind your proposed expedition and could apply to other expeditionary funding bodies to help raise the rest of the necessary cash. You could also approach people for sponsorship in goods with grovelling letters now bearing the Oxford University crest.

In the winter of 1954, sat in his bedroom in Magdalen College trying to write up his own expedition proposal, Bryan wasn't very hopeful that anything he put to the OUEC selection committee would meet with their approval:

Their task is not an easy one, for they are presented with many grandiloquent schemes, promising tremendous achievements at negligible cost.

With ideas and plans for the expedition still quite vague in Bryan's mind, he thought he should at least start to recruit some potential team members. When I spoke to him, he remembered:

> Bryan: "I sort of put out an advert at the Exploration Club, anybody want to come to Morocco kind of thing, and these various bods came. I did a certain amount of selecting because there was at least one person who shall remain nameless that I decided I wouldn't touch with a bargepole and he eventually went off and did a one-man expedition to South America…"

In contrast to when I was at Oxford, where most people came fresh from school with only the occasional Gap Year taker, by the time the students of the 1950s arrived at university, they were older, with broader life experience, as many had completed several years of National Service. Bryan himself had served with the Canadian Air Force, though admitted he was a very bad pilot. If his expedition to Morocco was to be successful, Bryan's team would need a wide range of useful skills, not least to be able to look after themselves.

> Bryan: "The only way we could get there was by driving, because otherwise it would be too expensive and so we needed a mechanic, and Peter Galloway was the person of choice. He'd been in the 17th/21st Lancers which is a cavalry regiment. The cavalry do tanks and trucks and things and he'd done a lot of work with mechanics. He was also a very stable nice man. We were also interested in making a detailed study of a tribal village and that's where Peter came in again because he was reading Geography, and so he knew all about mapping and things and he could map the village."

While having a geographer and mechanic on board was a good start, the core thrust of the expedition was still going to be some sort of biological survey, and while Bryan could cover the zoology angle, he needed a plant expert, or at least someone who knew something about plants.

> Bryan: "Of the botanists that turned up, the one that was most suitable was John Newbould. He had trained in botany and had been in the commandoes and that seemed like a very good combination."

While John sounded like an excellent person to have on the trip, he told Bryan he didn't suffer fools gladly, to which Bryan noted in his diary that he 'felt offended that he should be included in this category'. Bryan recalled that John also had a rather wild side:

> Bryan: "Several times he was in danger of being sent down from Merton College because he had run amok with a sword when he got drunk…"

The fourth member of the team was history student Humphrey Beckett, who Bryan felt could bring a bit of much-needed balance to the group. Humphrey was also interested in conducting ethnological studies of the Berber tribespeople.

> Bryan: "Humphrey Beckett was the dreamiest one of us, less practical but more imaginative. The most artistic and he was reading History and he wanted to do anthropology."

> Humphrey: "When I went to that first meeting of the Exploration Club, I think I was hoping to pick up a trip

going to Asia. But then I met Bryan Clarke and thought this sounded like an adventure too. I really knew very little about Morocco. I was looking for something with travel and adventure for the long vacation and it now happened to be Morocco. But important things followed from it which I hadn't envisaged when I went there."

The fifth member of the team was another zoologist, a final year student called Colin Pennycuick. Bryan went to see him:

Bryan: "Colin was something of a Bohemian, oblivious to personal discomfort and completely other-worldly. I remember his digs were an absolute shambles. Mind you, he was just fascinated by things biological…"

The five strong expedition team would also be joined briefly by Bryan's former schoolmate, Charles Pasternak, who had already completed his degree in chemistry at Oxford and had started a doctorate in biochemistry. With some input from his academic supervisor, Charles came up with the idea he could come out to Morocco midway through the expedition and try and study some facet of the blood chemistry of the native Berber tribes. He was hoping he might find an abnormality or two which he could write up.

With his expedition team assembled, all Bryan needed now was to get his expedition proposal past the aged Senior Council members of the OUEC.

Bryan's original plan for his summer expedition was, to put it mildly, wildly ambitious. In his initial pitch submitted to the OUEC Council, he proposed his team would travel ten thousand miles across North Africa, through Morocco, Algeria and Tunisia, collecting animals along the way, including a cheeky bit of scuba diving thrown in for good measure. Unsurprisingly, the

Expedition Council turned it down. Bryan took the rejection fairly on the chin and wrote:

Had not the council's disposal of our plans been so crushingly logical, I might well have abandoned altogether the idea of going to Morocco. As it was, I became mulishly determined to carry it through.

Taking note of their feedback, Bryan drastically scaled back his ambitions and worked on redrafting his expedition proposal. Turning to some maps he'd got out of the library, he focused his attention on a small region in the High Atlas Mountains of southern Morocco, centred on a village called Taddert. The area looked suitably remote and isolated, a perfect place to study the Berber people living there and the animals and plants that also called it home. He noted in his new proposal document that there was *a petrol station, telephone and a coaching house. We will leave the truck at Taddert and travel on foot to the selected village.*

The new location for the expedition was felt (by the OUEC Council) to be a much more manageable, localised site for the students to successfully conduct (and complete) a useful summer project, and indeed, an excellent place to study endemic wildlife, both flora and fauna. The Council also agreed there should be ample opportunity for the team to complete their additional objectives – a wide-reaching set of anthropological studies, including an investigation into the agriculture resource management in the chosen Berber village, along with a study into indigenous pottery techniques and possibly even the recording of some Berber tribal music. Part of the Council feedback on his original submission was to get input from the local authorities, so Bryan now included in his proposal some correspondence he'd had with a number of people in Morocco. His redrafted proposal triumphantly declared that *The Controleur Civil... has told us that he will instruct the local Berber chiefs to cooperate with us. He has also said that there is no political unrest in the area.*

The team was clearly led to believe (at least by the French authorities that Bryan had been in touch with) that all was well in Morocco. They didn't fully appreciate that come the summer, they would be entering a hotbed of political unrest and nationalistic fervour. Bryan later wrote:

> *We went to Morocco with little or no real knowledge of the political situation and our opinions grew from our own rather limited experiences... In some ways we had a unique opportunity to hear the views of both sides.*

While the occupying French forces effectively controlled the whole country, the area in the High Atlas that Bryan had chosen as the expedition's proposed study site fell under the jurisdiction of a Moroccan French sympathiser. His name was T'hami el Glaoui, the Pasha of Marrakech.

3

Lord of the Atlas

El Glaoui's full title was His Excellency Si El Hadj T'hami El Mezouari El Glaoui Le Pacha de Marrakech. Born in 1879, he was the son of a Berber tribal leader (the *Caid* of Telouet) and an Ethiopian concubine. T'hami and his older brother Madani (born 1866) started out as chiefs of what was just one of many Berber tribes that occupied the High Atlas Mountains, with their main fortified stronghold (or kasbah) located in the town of Telouet.

The family's rise to power began in 1893, when the Moroccan Sultan Moulay Hassan was on the march with his army, returning via Telouet from a campaign battling Berber warlords in the south. Some accounts say the army was defeated and starving, others that the campaign was successful, but the army got stranded in a mountain blizzard on their return. Either way, they were provided with food and shelter by Madani el Glaoui at his kasbah in Telouet. In payment, Madani was made *Khalifa* (the Sultan's representative) of the area and the brothers were given an arsenal of weapons, including a 77mm Krupp cannon.

This beast of a field gun could fire a 4kg projectile some 3000m. Its presentation to the Glaoui family proved to be a turning point in their family fortunes as they were now able to use the aforementioned cannon to blow holes in the assorted kasbahs of their own rival warlords. It set T'hami el Glaoui on the path to becoming the most powerful of all Berber warlords, and effective ruler of a great swathe of southern Morocco. During his lifetime, through his position and connections, T'hami also amassed great wealth and was thought to be one of the richest men on the planet.

With the arrival of the French in the late 1800s, and the beginning of what can only be described as the 'occupation' of Morocco (the French preferred 'pacification') in 1907, older brother Madani saw an opportunity to drive forward his political ambitions. By proclaiming that he was a close supporter of the French, the occupying French authorities made him Minister of War. T'hami was also elevated to Pasha of Marrakech, a position he would use both for political and financial gains.

On 30th March 1912, the Treaty of Fes was signed by Sultan Abd al-Hafid of Morocco and French diplomat Eugène Regnault. It was instigated by the Sultan, who was said to be struggling to maintain control over the different factions within Morocco, and by seeking help from the French, he hoped to regain control over his country. It was a complex agreement whereby the French would administer Morocco on behalf of the Moroccans. As I understand it, they also gained authority over non-Moroccan citizens, but the Moroccan government was promised they would still maintain control over their own citizens. However, not long after, direct rule by the French was imposed. France effectively used the Treaty to make Morocco a French colony (or 'Protectorate') with General Hubert Lyautey sworn in as the first French Resident General. When Madani el Glaoui died in 1918 (aged fifty-six), Lyautey nominated T'hami as head of the Glaoui family, bypassing Madani's sons. He requested T'hami raise an army by uniting the various Berber warlords of the Atlas region to subdue the troublesome tribes south of the Atlas, all under the umbrella of the French Protectorate. By 1935, pacification of the south was complete, with T'hami el Glaoui in control.

> Bryan: "When the French originally 'colonised' Morocco (I think they called it 'pacified'), there was a lot of warring factions and one very powerful warring faction was the el Glaoui family. They were quite well off because they controlled the passage over the Atlas Mountains, took tolls from people who wanted to go across. The French allied themselves to el Glaoui and the deal was he would help them. This was clearly a case of divide and rule because they reckoned that if you wanted to control the Arabs you used Berbers and vice versa. So they made a deal with el Glaoui and left him alone."

T'hami el Glaoui had his fingers in business interests right across the country, including a number of very lucrative cobalt and manganese mines. He built lavish palaces, such as the Dar el Bacha in the old medina of Marrakech, and his many kasbahs were now fortified, all paid for by the taxes Glaoui collected from his subjects. This included the growing trade and export of hashish, and what appeared to be a vast prostitution racket based out of Marrakech. The French were happy to let him get on with it in return for his continued support.

In his book *Lords of the Atlas*, Gavin Maxwell provides a bit of colour to T'hami's personal character, describing him as a serial womaniser, entertaining himself with a vast harem of girls. According to Maxwell, el Glaoui even had agents at train stations on the lookout for pretty European female travellers who would be greeted and given an invitation to a Glaoui palace. He built a golf course in the desert, entertained the rich and famous (including Charlie Chaplin and French author Colette) and became a bit of a celebrity on the world stage, boasting Winston Churchill as a friend.

In time, Bryan and his team would meet members of the Glaoui family, who would go on to provide letters of introduction, grant them assorted permissions to carry out their studies and even host the students at several of their lavish kasbahs. But the rise in the Nationalist movement in Morocco was starting to have a direct impact on this French-supporting *Lord of the Atlas*.

T'hami el Glaoui
Historic Collection / Alamy Stock Photo

4

Planning

With his newly rewritten expedition proposal now approved by the OUEC Council, Bryan applied to other funding bodies to raise the money he needed for his Moroccan adventure:

> Bryan: "It was put to the Royal Geographical Society as one of the official university expeditions and we got some money from them. I then wrote to National Geographic magazine and I wrote to all kinds of people asking for free things that we conned people into supplying to us."

Bryan was rather bold when seeking sponsorship, with no qualms about going straight to the top. On 1st March 1955, he wrote to his mother:

> *Life is extremely busy at the moment. This expedition takes an awful lot of organising. I have just written to Sir Winston Churchill. It will be interesting to see whether I get a reply or am immediately thrown in jail.*

Letter from Bryan to his Mother, March 1955

In his book, Bryan later recalled:

This piece of impertinence elicited a very polite and forbearing reply from one of his secretaries. The envelope was marked '10 Downing Street' and in heavy type

'PRIME MINISTER'. It rested for some days in the college letter rack and created a mild sensation among my friends.

Despite receiving a rejection from Winston Churchill, others were happy to help and slowly the supplies came in, with his college bedroom acting as storeroom:

> *One armchair came to house ten boxes of penicillin, two prismatic compasses, a small hatchet, forty feet of rope and a large supply of toilet paper. The other groaned under a 76-pound crate of tinned margarine... we had become 'The Oxford University Expedition to Southern Morocco'. Later on, signing cheques and documents, I came to regret the length of the title, but in this moment it seemed very important and impressive.*

Sifting through the amassed collection of papers and receipts that Bryan had kept from the expedition, I stumbled upon various replies he'd received to what would have been countless begging letters asking for supplies (for free, or at least at discounted prices). One from Imperial Chemical Industries (now more commonly known as ICI) detailed how the company would be happy to supply a range of pharmaceuticals, listing (along with penicillin) things like Carbon Tetrachloride, Sulphamezathine and Paradichlorobenzene crystals. The letter went on to apologise, saying that it could not help with Bryan's request for a large supply of margarine, noting that ICI did not in fact manufacture said spread, but suggested instead that Bryan contact a company called Van den Berghs Ltd in the hope of filling this void. A reply from Van den Berghs (Hospital and Catering Service) indicated they were happy to supply the expedition's margarine needs and detailed how they recommended putting the 76lbs (34kg) they were donating in 7½ oz tins for ease of transport and storage.

Maps were sourced from Blackwells, the gigantic bookstore on Oxford's Broadstreet, and company Emberlin and Son on Turl Street in the heart of the city provided the expedition's stationary, including a thousand sheets of Eden Grove Bond paper, inscribed with 'O.U. Expedition to Southern Morocco', along with the Oxford University crest.

As well as raising funds and securing supplies for the expedition, Bryan also continued to research more about the political situation in Morocco. He took receipt of assorted pamphlets which, contrary to the correspondence he'd had with various French officials based in Morocco, appeared to paint quite a bleak picture. One reported how a French police car was driving through a bazaar in Casablanca when it opened fire. It noted:

> *These moors were not fleeing or resisting arrest. They were shopping peacefully. Three died. Three were hurt. French terror was teaching the Moors a lesson.*

News was also coming out of Morocco of acts of torture under the French administration. The pamphlet described how *the French know how to use terror in Morocco. It is part and parcel of their political tactics.* Bryan later wrote that:

> *These pamphlets caused me some concern. Whether they were true or false, it was clear that all was not well.*

The Nationalist movement in Morocco had (in some form) been around since the late 1800s, when French, Spanish and other European nations started to occupy parts of the country, but it really took off in the 1920s with the rise of the Istiqlal (Independence) Party. Its manifesto was clear:

> *The essential condition for the revival of Morocco is its*

*independence, because a country unable to enjoy the
various attributes of sovereignty is inevitably destined to
remain the slave of that which holds it down.*

By 1950, a mutual suspicion and animosity had grown between
Sultan Mohammed V Ben Youssef and the wealthy and powerful
T'hami el Glaoui, Pasha of Marrakech. By some reports, el
Glaoui did not think the country was ready for independence
as it was not yet unified. By January 1951, relations between the
French (and by association, el Glaoui) and Sultan Mohammed V
had further worsened. The French asked the Sultan to denounce
the Istiqlal party. He refused and so the French (momentarily)
severed all contact with the Sultan. Glaoui also helped stir up
trouble by sending an army of Berbers to make a surprise attack
on Fes and the country's capital Rabat.

Throughout 1951 and 1952, the continued rise of the
Nationalist movement caused increased instability throughout
Morocco. While relations were resumed between the French
authorities and the Sultan, all pro-Istiqlal reporting was banned,
hence the restricted (and censored) information coming out
of Morocco. Mass arrests of prominent nationalists followed,
but protests were now flaring up right across the country. On
7th December 1952, a riot in Casablanca was halted when the
French sprayed the gathered crowds with machine gun fire –
this was the atrocity noted in the pamphlet Bryan had been sent.

Meanwhile, el Glaoui routed out nationalist sympathisers
from his own tribe and in January 1953, rallied the Berber tribes
of the south to denounce the Istiqlal and the Sultan. This in turn,
upset the country's religious rulers, and in August 1953, Glaoui
found himself excommunicated by the country's religious court.
But that didn't stop him still holding immense power over a
large chunk of the country.

With news of the growing turmoil in Morocco gradually

finding its way to Oxford, the University authorities were becoming a little concerned about sending a group of their students off to a country in such a potential state of turmoil. But with media outlets strongly censored by the French, the truth on the ground and the scale of the unrest was difficult to properly ascertain.

> Bryan: "It was clear there was quite a lot of politics that we didn't want to be involved in, and anyway, we were pretty ignorant."

Over the coming months, supplies for the expedition kept coming in, but the situation in Morocco did not appear to be getting any better. There was now some pressure for the expedition to be called off.

> Humphrey: "The British Consul General in Tangier whose son was on my staircase in Worcester College had strongly advised the University against our going. He said, 'the situation is blowing up and it could be dangerous and these chaps could simply be a cause of great anxiety to the British and French Authorities. They shouldn't go'. But we went anyway."

Unperturbed, and with the University still giving them the green light, by late June 1955, the group of students were preparing to set off. Rather than fly (far too costly) and acquire a vehicle in Morocco, the plan was to drive all the way from Oxford to the Atlas Mountains (and back again). For the princely sum of £55, they bought an old ex-Canadian army Fordson 2-ton truck, formerly used on the estate of the Marquess of Bath. From the looks of one very detailed receipt I found from Hartwells of Oxford (Automobile Engineers), the truck needed a lot of remedial work (costing more than three times the original price of the truck itself) and many parts had to be replaced to get it ready to make such a long journey.

The days leading up to their departure were fraught with anxieties, not so much about the news of bombs and bloodshed, but about packing. Bryan wrote in his book that:

Peter fared worst of all. When the time came for packing, we assembled everything in his rooms at Merton. It was an expedition in itself to reach the bed.

Humphrey: "There it all was around the floor of his rooms and we needed to get a Customs Officer to put the seals on all the boxes. We thought this would finish by 5pm. We actually finished at 1am, so by then the college gate was locked and we had to hoist the Customs Officer over the railings of Merton College. He was a very decent fellow and took it all in good part. He was fairly drunk by this time as we'd fed him scotch or whatever all evening and so we hoisted the chap over. Then Peter went off somewhere else and actually left me in his bedroom to sleep over. When his Scout came in the next morning, he opened the bedroom door and saw somebody other than Peter in the bed. He said, 'Excuse me sir I wouldn't go to breakfast if I were you…' and this was the sole rebuke for the fact there was a stranger in Peter's room."

The team needed to compartmentalise all their supplies into smallish packages so that, when they arrived in the mountains, they could be decanted into panniers slung on the backs of mules – I thought this was excellent forward thinking on the team's part. Bryan explained in his book how the answer to the problem came by way of the college cellars:

*A solution was found in the use of champagne boxes...
thus our equipment came to be packed in a series of
containers, each with a large label reading Moet &
Chandon. This gave rise to some caustic comments about
what we considered to be essential supplies.*

On the morning of 30th June 1955, Bryan remembered being
woken by his landlady Mrs Bell. He wrote in his diary *Mrs Bell
said, 'Oh you're going to Morocco today, Mr Clarke, I must make
you some sandwiches'.*

That afternoon, the team mounted up and drove off, leaving
the dreaming spires of Oxford behind. But even before they left
British soil, they encountered a problem:

Humphrey: "We were very late setting off to Dover and I
think we got there in the early hours of the morning. But
the truck was an ex-army truck and was khaki in colour
and we knew that given the current situation in Morocco,
it wasn't a good idea to be travelling in something that
looked anything like an army vehicle. On the customs
documents for the journey, it was described as grey, but
we had forgotten to repaint it. So we frantically painted
the truck grey in the early hours, and with the paintwork
still tacky, we drove onto the ferry."

With the truck now freshly painted, the group felt it needed a
name. At the time, Humphrey was reading the works of French
novelist Alphonse Daudet. His 1872 novel featured a plump,
middle-aged man called Tartarin de Tarascon. Tartarin set
out on adventures to hunt big game in North Africa, but after
gathering a mass of equipment and weapons, he hooks up with
a conman posing as a Prince and his gullibility leads him on a
number of misadventures, but ultimately, he achieved nothing.

Humphrey, with his dry wit, decided to name the truck *Tartarin* after the hero of the novel. After months of preparation, the expedition finally left Britain.

5

In Their Footsteps

Five decades later, in early 2007, I started to plan my own expedition to Morocco to try and follow in the students' footsteps. I began sorting through all my accumulated research notes and the bulging folder of source materials and photos provided by the original expedition members. My immediate goal was to try and locate the Berber village they had studied up in the High Atlas Mountains and then work out how to get there.

Unlike the students back in 1955, who set off to study an as yet undesignated 'Berber village', I had the benefit of Bryan's book and knew where I wanted to go prior to leaving the UK. The name of the village that became the focus of their studies was called Idirh, located in the Ait Rbaa valley. Sadly, the name Idirh didn't jump out from any Google searches (except when referring to Bryan's book) and didn't get a mention in any guide books, nor could I find any reference to the Ait Rbaa. But rummaging through Bryan's notes, I unearthed a hand-drawn map of the region which, rather crudely, showed the location of the village. It suggested that the valley in which Idirh was to be found was located between two places, one called Taddert (which Bryan had mentioned in his expedition proposal) and Telouet (which I now knew was the site of el Glaoui's formidable kasbah). Fortunately, both sites showed up on my internet searches. Sadly, the map gave no useful clues (other than a dotted line) as to how one journeyed from either Taddert or Telouet into the mountain valley itself, yet at least I now had two known points from which to triangulate my search. For the time being, that was as far as I could get with pinpointing the actual location of the village itself, so I turned my attention to travel logistics.

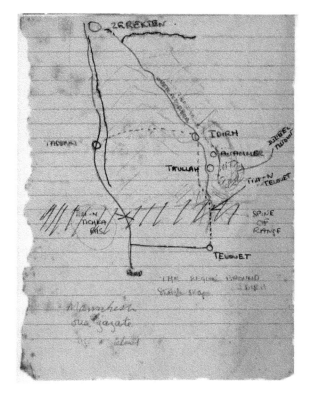

Bryan's hand-drawn map identifying the location of the
Berber Village of Idirh

By this time, I had managed to rope in my nephew James to come and join me on my journey of rediscovery. James was a twenty-three-year-old barman (he'd prefer 'Food and Beverage Manager') at a private health club. He lived with his parents not far from me and so we would see each other quite often. The promise of a jaunt off into the unknown appealed to him as much as it did to me.

As far as my professional life was going, I was just finishing a large landmark BBC television series exploring how the Earth works, called *Earth: The Power of the Planet*, presented by geologist Prof Iain Stewart. Our episode was investigating how the Earth's inner heat helped (and still helps) shape the continents through tectonic and volcanic activity. We'd flown out to the Afar region of Ethiopia (in a rickety old ex-Russian military helicopter) to an active volcano called Erta Ale (part of the Great Rift Valley), where we stared down into a lake of molten lava. We'd been to the South Island of New Zealand to experience the tectonic uplift of the New Zealand Alps, flown around by one of the helicopter pilots who had worked on *Lord of the Rings* (mid-ride he quipped, "Just over there, I dropped off Gandalf…"), and then onto the North Island, to the stinking mud pits of Rotorua. We had a quick jaunt to film Mt Etna in Sicily (sadly, low clouds obscured the audibly erupting volcano) and even scuba-dived between the American and Eurasian tectonic plates in Iceland, shivering in glacial melt water that barely reached two degrees Celsius. The edit had gone well, and my episode was to be the first in the series, so I now had time available to organise our Moroccan adventure.

As our trip to Morocco was effectively going to be first contact (for us at least) with the Berber tribespeople, I decided that we would benefit from having a local Berber speaking guide. While Bryan's rough hand-drawn map was useful to locate the valley, it gave no means to actually navigate a route to the specific Berber village of Idirh that we were aiming for. I felt that a Berber guide would not only give us a fighting chance of actually finding Idirh, but also, would allow us to communicate with the local inhabitants and ask them if they or any of their relatives remembered the university students coming to live with them all those years ago. I also wanted to see if we could identify any of the people in the cache of old photographs I had been given by the original expedition members and to investigate in what ways the village had changed or stayed the same over the last fifty years. My spoken French ability was a bit rusty (my GCSE exams had been completed some eighteen years earlier), but I found I could still get by with conversational French, as long as everyone stayed in the present tense. But I doubted the Berber villagers spoke much French, and sadly my Arabic was limited to *Salaam Alaikum* which, while this would fulfil a useful role as a polite greeting, wasn't going to get us very far with our investigations.

A quick internet search led me to a Moroccan-based travel company and, following a brief phone call, they assured me they had the facilities to organise both transportation and a Berber speaking guide to lead us (by foot) up into the mountains. The person confidently told me that they knew the various villages of the region we wished to visit. They also mentioned that the villages were still only accessible by a very rough dirt track leading into and out of the valley from the main road, and so, just as people had done for centuries, we would have to walk in, but they should be able to arrange a mule to carry our bags. The tour company agreed to pick us up from Marrakech, drive us to the village of Taddert, then our guide would lead us into the mountains where they would also source some local accommodation for us in the village of Idirh itself. Having stayed in the village and achieved our goals, the guide would then lead us back out of the mountain valley to the village of

Telouet (home to that imposing kasbah), where we would then have a car arranged to take us on to a town called Ouarzazate. At this point, I thought we should be able to hire our own car to further investigate some of the other destinations the original expedition members went on to explore.

Unlike the university students back in 1955, I didn't have the luxury (though I doubt they thought it was a 'luxury') of having the time to drive all the way down from England to Morocco. While they had had adventures along the way (many of which involved their truck breaking down), for me, the focus of my trip wasn't about *getting* to Morocco, it was about *finding* the Berber village and seeing how the villagers' way of life had changed or stayed the same since the time the students made camp there. To this end, I booked flights to take me and James direct to Marrakech, whereupon our adventure would begin in earnest.

6

Travelling through Morocco

Back in 1955, having cleared customs and caught the ferry from Dover, the five students arrived in Calais and started the long drive down through France and Spain. The journey gave them opportunity to get to know each other. But it was far from an easy drive as their truck suffered several breakdowns.

Bryan: "We really got very ratty with each other and on occasion we thought it was all going to collapse before we even got there. We had all these breakdowns and it was very annoying and the temperature was 110."

Fortunately, the quarrels soon died down and the team started to gel together. Reaching Gibraltar, they stayed a night as guests of the British Governor. Bryan noted in his diary that the rooms had chamber pots emblazoned with 'GR' in gold (I assume that was King George VI?). A day or so later, they crossed over to Morocco on a car ferry named *Mons Calpe* and, meeting with a Mrs Dunlop at the British consulate in Tangier, were invited to stay the night, setting up camp on the consulate veranda.

At this time, Tangier was governed by an International Committee of Control made up of representatives from Britain, Netherlands, USA, France, Spain, Portugal, Belgium and Italy. When I spoke to Bryan, he referred to the situation as a 'diplomatocracy' as all the power was in the hands of the European diplomats.

It was here they bumped into travel writer Peter Mayne. In 1949, Peter had moved to Morocco to live among the locals and then, in 1953, published his first book, *The Alleys of Marrakesh* (Bryan had a well-thumbed hardback edition of the book in his luggage). In his book, Peter gave a vivid first-person account of his experience of living in Morocco, the place, the people and the politics. His wonderfully evocative, sometimes a little sardonic but often romantic picture of what life was like had inspired Bryan when writing up his expedition proposal, and it was Bryan's own copy of Peter's book that I read to see what sort of insights he may have taken from it.

Peter wrote that there was no point in making any sort of plans in Morocco *as if you were a free agent in the matter*, going on to explain the notion of *insha'Allah*. He noted that whether someone did something for you (or turned up at the appointed place or time etc.) depended on whether the thing requested of them gave them *comfort or livelihood or advantage*. He went on to write that when asked to do something, *if the thing has no importance, which is taken to mean that it has no real bearing upon your personal prosperity or pleasure, you may quite easily find that something outside your control prevents you doing whatever it is*. I'll return to *insha'Allah* and this way of living and thinking a bit later on.

Now sitting with the team at the consulate in Tangier, Peter gave them some brief lessons in Moroccan protocol. Bryan wrote:

He told us about the observances of Moorish society,
how many cups of mint tea to drink, the correct forms of
address to persons of different rank, the method of eating
Kus Kus and so on.

Knowledge of polite formalities would certainly help the
students get by, but of far greater concern at that time was the
changing political landscape. Some commentators strongly
believed the rise of the Moroccan Nationalist movement meant
that the country was on the verge of collapse.

At the turn of the twentieth century, Morocco was ruled by
a Sultan named Abd al-Aziz. But across the country, there were
many inter-tribal wars and skirmishes, with many tribes declaring
themselves independent of the Sultan. In 1908, Abd al-Aziz was
deposed to be replaced by his brother Abd al-Hafid. It was during
his tumultuous four years in power that he called on the French
to restore order to the country. As I mentioned earlier, in March
1912, the Treaty of Fes was signed between France and Morocco.
General Lyautey was sworn in as the first Resident General and
Morocco became a French Protectorate, with Yusef Ben Hassan
(another of Abd al-Hafid's brothers) becoming Sultan.

Under the French Protectorate, a new government was
appointed and major engineering projects were set in motion,
including the construction of ports, roads and railways. With the
help of T'hami el Glaoui (newly appointed in his role as Pasha
of Marrakech), the French authorities made plans to subdue the
warring Berber tribes of the south. To try and bring the Berbers
under control, on 16th May 1930, the French passed the Berber
Decree (*Berber Dahir*) which, among other things, allowed the
various tribes to use their own traditional methods of justice,
as opposed to being under the direct control of the Sultan or
the state (and Islamic Sharia law). This was seen by many as
an act to divide the Moroccan people, driving a split between

'Arab' and 'Berber'. Protest against the Decree (and the ongoing presence of the French authorities) helped build support for the growing Moroccan Nationalist movement and the formation of the Nationalist Istiqlal Party.

In 1927, Mohammed Ben Youssef (Mohammed V) became Sultan, following the death of his father Sultan Yusef Ben Hassan. While the new Sultan initially supported the French, he later switched sides to favour the Nationalists. As a result, on 20th August 1953, the French/Glaoui alliance managed to exile him to Corsica (then on to Madagascar), and a puppet Sultan (Mohammed Ben Aarafa) was placed on the throne. Aarafa effectively signed over control to the French and Glaoui.

By the summer of 1955 and the arrival of the students from Oxford, the country was like a tinder box ready to explode. And explode it did in certain regions, with bombs and bloodshed. Bryan wrote in his book:

Morocco at the time of our arrival was in a very unsettled state… we were told about the dangers for Europeans to enter medinas of any Moroccan town as Nationalist feeling was high.

Leaving the safety of the British consulate in Tangier, on 14th July, the team continued their journey south. But as the sun set one evening, their truck *Tartarin* broke down (again) – it was this event that Bryan had recounted in the first chapter of his book. The students needed to catch a lift to the nearest motor garage to get help in making repairs, but they couldn't work out why nobody would stop, or even slow down for that matter. Eventually, a policeman on a motorbike pulled up.

Humphrey: "Peter and Colin were the main mechanics. They couldn't get the truck going. So two of us were trying to hitch a lift to the next town and see if we could get a mechanic to come out and help us. We stood beside the road thumbing a lift and as it happened what pulled up was a French Corporal of the Gendarmerie, heavily armed, followed by an ambulance and behind that another motorcycle policeman. We explained the situation to the policeman who said 'OK, get in the ambulance'. So he opened up the doors and there were two very bloody individuals on stretchers. Back up the road where we'd come from, bombs or grenades had been thrown and these two unfortunates were injured and being taken to hospital. The Corporal got them to move over and shoved us in, and they took us to the town. We found a garage and incidentally the garage man (a Frenchman) wasn't enthusiastic about coming out. We were just standing discussing the situation wondering what to do when the truck pulled up – they'd got it going again."

Unknown to the team, that night a bomb had gone off in Casablanca, killing and wounding Moroccans and Europeans alike. This subsequently triggered three days of riots and brutal reprisals by the French. According to the official casualty list, there were at least 35 Moroccan and 11 European deaths, plus 218 Moroccans and 88 Europeans seriously wounded. Unaware of the wider scale of growing unrest, the team continued their journey down to Morocco's capital city Rabat.

Just as I had done decades later, Bryan realised early on that the team would need a Berber speaking interpreter to provide open communication channels when in the mountains. En route, they had arranged to pick up an eighteen-year-old Berber student who would journey with the group and act as their translator. His name was Mouhsine M'Barek and he was studying at the Berber college in the town of Azrou. Humphrey would later write that M'Barek was *a cheerful mountain boy whose brains have taken him to college... he has the impression that anything can happen with a party of crazy Englishmen and has endeavoured to provide for all possible and some improbable occasions.*

In Rabat, they also had an appointment with the French authorities (with whom they'd had some correspondence during the planning stages of the trip) to arrange their final permissions to venture into the High Atlas. Given what was going on in the country at that moment, I was surprised they weren't sent packing, but somehow the relevant permissions were granted, and that evening they stayed overnight, sleeping in the relative safety of the garden of the British Consulate. The following day, the British Consular General thought it pertinent to write them a letter of introduction to help facilitate their travels and addressed it to none other than the Pasha of Marrakech himself, T'hami el Glaoui.

Throughout 1955, the history books reveal that el Glaoui was involved in many a backroom deal with the French authorities governing Morocco. On the day of the Casablanca bombing (14th July), he had been invited to lunch by the new French Resident General, Gilbert Grandval. Glaoui was pushing for the French forces to restore order and get their puppet Sultan Aarafa out and about and seen by the people. Sadly, two assassination attempts on his life had encouraged Aarafa to stay behind closed, guarded doors. Grandval found himself in a bit of a quandary. With the continuing rise of the Nationalist movement across the country, the Moroccan people were now calling for the return of the exiled Sultan Mohammed V. At the same time, Grandval was even being encouraged by the French government in Paris to allow the Sultan's return, to help try and restore order. But on the other hand, Grandval had el Glaoui (backed by his army of

Berbers) insisting Mohammed V should stay in exile. This would allow the Pasha to carry on effectively ruling half of Morocco in the style of his choosing. Also, if Aarafa did step down, Glaoui told Grandval that Sultan Mohammed V would almost certainly join with the Nationalist Istiqlal voices and push for the eviction of the French. As a result, Grandval delayed any action, except to ensure any rioting or unrest was brutally dealt with, as witnessed in the city of Fes on 25th July, where French police once again opened fire on a crowd.

Meanwhile, what seemed like a universe away from the riots and bloodshed, the students attended a cocktail party at the British Consulate. Bryan noted that the Consular General informed them *The Pasha was well disposed towards the English, probably because of his association with Sir Winston Churchill.* Unknown to Bryan, T'hami el Glaoui had often entertained Churchill at his palace (Dar el Bacha) in Marrakech. Churchill was a prodigious painter and would often paint with el Glaoui's son Hassan, who I discovered had gone on to become one of Morocco's most famous figurative painters. Churchill even invited the Pasha to be his guest at the coronation of Queen Elizabeth II back in June 1953. It was reported that T'hami came bearing all manner of gifts, hoping (it's said) that he would be granted a knighthood, but all his presents were refused, as gifts could only be accepted from Heads of State, of which he wasn't.

Unperturbed by the roadside dramas, and with no real knowledge of the widespread extent of the turbulent politics currently tearing the country apart, the team drove on, down through Morocco. Finally, they arrived at Marrakech.

7

Arrival in Marrakech

In his 1953 book *The Alleys of Marrakesh*, Peter Mayne gave a flavour of what life was like living (by his own admission) a 'back street life' in the famous red city. He painted a picture of a *frenzy of sound…and whirlpools of activity* and the promise of *an animated, noisy, crowded, perpetual fairground*. He went on to write how Marrakech had *a tideless sea, waves of djellaba hordes, a flecking of skullcaps moving closely together, so close that identities merge into the general turbulence*.

For Gavin Maxwell in his 1966 book *Lords of the Atlas*, it was the sounds as well as the sights of Marrakech that caught his attention:

> *The sound of human voices comes up like the muted rumble of some vast engine, an undertone to the perpetual staccato urgency of drums, the wailing of reed pipes, the clanging of symbols, the shrill tinkle of water sellers' bells, the endless calling of the beggars.*

He continued:

Snake charmers and sword swallowers and fire eaters... gaudily dressed acrobats from Taroudant forming towers of multicoloured unidentifiable limbs, conjurers and mimes and storytellers... Berber dancers from the mountains, their white robed lines swaying in rhythmic advance and withdrawal.

All very evocative stuff, and quite a feast for all the senses. For the five dusty, already travel-weary students approaching the city, the magic of Marrakech did not escape them. Bryan later wrote:

The first sight of Marrakech was genuinely exciting... there was an increasing stream of traffic. Cars and carts, donkeys and camels, men and women. All of them staggering under huge loads of merchandise.

Arriving at the city was one thing, but gaining entry was another. As they made their final approach, the team headed to a massive stone gateway built into the huge city walls. Standing guard, a soldier waved them to a halt, saying it was not permitted to enter the medina due to 'events'. Unknown to the team, there had been riots in the city on the very day they arrived, and Europeans living in the Old Quarter were being evacuated to the European Quarter, known as the Gueliz. Initially, Bryan tried to get a room at the American Red Cross, but they were not let in. As night was drawing in, the group decided to stay outside the ancient city walls, camping in the nearby palm groves. But this was not without its own problems:

Bryan: "These people came up and they said you can't camp here, you'll be killed. And we said, well we haven't got anywhere else to go and so these nice Moroccans said alright we'll stand guard. They stayed up all night guarding us and we got a bit spooked by this."

In his book, Bryan noted:

We arranged ourselves in defensive positions. Colin was stationed on top of the truck, Peter slept in the cab and John was underneath. I lay in the back armed with a large (and probably ineffective) knife.

The following morning, he wrote in his diary:

We had a slightly restless night – expecting to be attacked at any moment, but nothing happened...

Looking out at a view before them that had remained unchanged for centuries, he continued:

Camel caravans which had spent the night outside the city walls were getting under way for the final stage of their journey. Hooded figures were tightening loads on the backs of their beasts, while others brewed coffee or tea. The smoke from their fires rose straight in the cool morning air.

Their truck was eventually allowed to enter the city, and they drove to the central square, known as the Djemaa el-Fna, which translates as the 'Concourse of Sinners'. It was here in the square, not so many years before the students' arrival, that Sultans (and the Pasha of Marrakech) would display the severed heads of criminals and rebels, or in the case of the Pasha, anyone that he didn't like. Bryan was swept up by the sights and smells:

*The square houses traders of all kinds, vendors of spices
and herbs or bread, fruit and meat, medicine men, barbers,
confidence tricksters, letter writers, storytellers, snake
charmers, singers, dancers, pimps… a smooth tongued
and quick fingered gentleman was extracting money from
innocent bystanders with a variant of 'spot the card'… its
markets are famous throughout the world not only for the
variety on sale (one can buy anything from an aphrodisiac
to a motor car) but also for its astonishing collection of the
races and colours of men.*

But on that morning, the atmosphere was distinctly uneasy and
anti-French feeling was running very high. When I spoke to
Bryan, he recalled:

Bryan: "People were very unfriendly when we went
about Marrakech. They would spit, and they could
spit with great accuracy and they would spit behind
you as you were walking along. They thought we were
Frenchmen and people were really not very nice then,
they were instantly hostile."

Ignoring this open hostility, the team settled in to enjoy the
sights and sounds that have gripped this famous square for
centuries and still continue to excite and enrapture to this day.

Bryan: "In the evening all these paraffin lamps came
on, and strange Moroccan music. I mean it was so
atmospheric this place. There was a café there on the
edge of the square where you could either sit at the tables
on the pavement and look out or you could go up on the
roof where you could look down on it and that was a
sight. These masses of people all kinds of stuff going on.

It was a real Arabian Nights kind of place."

Bryan and his team had found their way to a restaurant known as the Café de France, which boasted a famous roof garden, and for the moment, we'll leave them there, enjoying some mint tea.

***

I had been to Marrakech once before – back in 1990, aged seventeen – when I went on an adventure overland trip, travelling right around the country with the tour group Exodus. Exodus was very much an economy adventure travel outfit, cheaper compared to the other providers at the time and, as a result, a little rough around the edges. We travelled in the back of a truck (not unlike *Tartarin* I suspect but a bit bigger and benefiting from being far more roadworthy), cooked our own food and camped out for most of the trip, which covered a great chunk of Morocco. Beginning in Marrakech, we headed out to the coastal cities of Essaouira and El Jadida, then inland and up to Rabat, Meknes and Fes (we bypassed Casablanca – unlike in the film starring Humphrey Bogart, it looked like a nasty industrial site from the main motorway), then down to the High Atlas Mountains and the edges of the Sahara, before circling back to Marrakech.

Back in 1990, my first impressions of the city pretty much matched everyone else's for the last two hundred years or so – the noise and smells, the people, the hassle and the vibrant chaos. As a nascent naturalist (at that time applying to study biology at Oxford), my diary made note of all the animals I saw while wandering around the square, most notably the snakes:

With their skin in tatters, the cobras are pulled around by the snake charmers for the crowds to gawp at and then shoved back in small boxes.

The monkeys didn't rate much higher, which I commented on being *dirty and scabby*. Wandering out into the souks located just off the square, I found that each shop appeared to sell exactly the same things, notably the djellabas (flowing Moroccan gowns) and the hubble-bubble pipes, two things every tourist must have (apparently). My initial observations were far less poetic than Peter Mayne's or Bryan's, but then I was midway through sixth form and hardly a refined diarist at that time. However, flicking to the back of my diary and our return to Marrakech (having spent three weeks touring Morocco), there was a different sentiment. While it appeared I still wasn't the biggest fan of Marrakech, writing, *so expensive and demanding. Much preferred every other town and city in Morocco.* But a paragraph later, my youthful heart appeared to have softened, as my concluding note referred to Marrakech as a *lovely town* and my final exploration around the chaotic mass of humanity just before we flew home was noted as being *too nice for words.*

My diary entries also recorded that I had found the legendary Café de France (still bearing the same name) and I wrote how I enjoyed a drink sat out on the balcony (as everyone does), taking photos of the various water sellers, snake charmers and monkeys out in the Djemaa el-Fna without them noticing and so not requiring any payment. Now seventeen years older, I was interested in how I would react to returning to the city and its famous square.

Landing at Marrakech airport, James and I had an intriguing run-in with the passport control man. He asked about my job and, revealing I was a television Producer/Director, he asked what television channel I worked for. I said the BBC, which was something he approved of. My baggage was delayed for a little while, but when it finally arrived, we were then pulled over by the customs man so that our bags could be scanned. The man wanted to take a look inside and was a bit bothered by the discovery of a sleeping bag. Looking in James's bag, he then got very excitable with the discovery of our map.

"Where is the Sahara?" he asked.

"I'm not sure," I replied.

He handed the map over to his superior, who explained that the map was wrong. He was pointing to an area just to the south of Morocco labelled as 'Western Sahara'.

"There is no such thing as *Western Sahara*. That is Morocco!" He was very insistent.

I said, "I agree. Yes, all Morocco."

I didn't know it at the time, but 'Western Sahara' is a hotly disputed swathe of land/country bordered by the Atlantic to the west, Mauritania to the east and south, and Morocco to the north. A former Spanish colony, it is one of the most sparsely populated territories in the world, but that didn't stop Morocco and Mauritania both laying claim to it (Morocco since 1957) and even going to war over it (in 1975) when Spain relinquished administrative control. In 1979, Mauritania withdrew its claim, leaving Morocco in control of most of the territory. A nationalist movement also exists in the form of the Sahrawi Arab Democratic Republic (SADR), with a government currently in exile in Algeria. To put it bluntly, it's a highly contentious area whose sovereignty clearly irked the customs official.

Satisfied that our map was not some sort of illicit document, we were eventually sent on our way, but now there was a big queue for the money change. We weren't allowed to take currency into or out of the country and so this was the first place we could get some Moroccan dirhams.

With cash now in hand, I had planned to take a cab into town and was reliably informed by my guidebook that a taxi would be fifty dirhams. On presenting this expectation to the cab drivers, we were told that that price was for each person and only for the multi-person 'big taxi' (i.e. not a private transfer), for which we would have to wait a while for it to fill up before it would depart. As is the norm (and indeed expectation) in Morocco, you have to barter for pretty much any purchase, and I wasn't going to let it go that easily – we bartered him down from 150 to 130 dirhams for the two of us and off we went. Not a big win, but a win all the same (sort of).

Although we had asked to be taken to our hotel, we were dropped off at the very edge of the Djemaa el-Fna as the taxi driver said he was not able to take us down the narrow alleys which would lead to our night's accommodation. Now on foot, we skirted round the southern edge of the square and off down one of the many alleys, walking past a grisly display of animal brains all laid out in a butcher's shop.

Our digs for the night was the Hotel Sherazade, a modest establishment in the style of a 'humble' riad or typical Moroccan house (as opposed to the deluxe riads that are now found in the city's New Quarter). I had sourced this rather budget outfit on the internet while planning our trip. The reception lady handed us the key to room eleven and we climbed the stairs. All the rooms were located around a central, open, tiled courtyard with a small bubbly fountain in the middle, surrounded by potted palm trees and other assorted shrubbery. Our room was very clean and cosy, but basic as befitted the rate. We now had the rest of the day to explore the city, as our pickup to take us to the mountains had been arranged for the following morning.

We decided to avoid the famous Djemaa el-Fna just for the moment and take in some of the city's other notable attractions – after all, it was still quite early in the day. There would be time to sample the delights of the legendary 'Concourse of Sinners' a little later. First stop was the Koutoubia, located just off the square and unmistakable due to its vast minaret.

I discovered that the Koutoubia is the largest mosque in the city, and its dazzling white minaret tower (completed in 1195) stands 77m tall, dominating the city skyline. This is the second mosque to bear that name – we explored the ruins of the first mosque which were neatly laid out just by the side of the current building. Apparently, the medieval builders adjusted the orientation of the second mosque to better align with the qibla, the direction of the Sacred Mosque in Mecca. As non-Muslims, we weren't allowed inside but did enjoy the green oasis of the nearby garden.

Next stop on our whirlwind tour of Marrakech was the kasbah area, entering through the massive twelfth century Bab Agnaou (*bab* just means gate). It was here that we came across the highly ornate Saadian Tombs, a royal necropolis dating from the late 1500s. The tombs were set in a large garden cemetery, and I discovered that it was down to the French that they were in such good nick. Having fallen out of use in the late eighteenth century, they were rediscovered in 1917 by the Service des Beaux-Arts, Antiquités et Monuments Historiques, who carefully restored them back to their former glory. The many different highly decorated chambers and ornate loggias were quite beautiful in the morning sunlight.

Just around the back of the Royal Palace (now a private residence), we stumbled upon the massive ruins of the Palais el Badi. Again, this dated from the late 1500s and the name translates as either the 'Palace of Wonder' or the 'Incomparable Palace'. Back in the day, this was a reception building where the Sultan hosted and received guests. While much of the marble and onyx was stripped from the site when it fell into decline, the astonishing craftsmanship was still clearly visible.

Finally, to the Palais de la Bahia. I thought it looked very much like the Alhambra of Granada in southern Spain with lots of ornate Koranic engravings, lots of tiles and a fabulously ornate ceiling. Compared to the other sites we'd visited in the city, this was a much more recent addition to Marrakech, built in the late nineteenth century. In 1908, Madani el Glaoui (T'hami's brother) took up residence in the Palais and used it to entertain foreign guests. But then, in 1912, following the signing of the Treaty of Fes, the palace was given over to become the residence of the French Resident General Hubert Lyautey. After independence, it once again became a royal residence for King Mohammed V, before being opened to the nation as a tourist attraction. Alongside the decoration and fine architecture, this palace boasted some striking courtyards to wander through.

Walking around the city's backstreets, it was fairly devoid of people (it was still early). As you'd expect, the European influences were quite prominent in the New Quarter, especially in the style and architecture of many of the buildings and in the layout and look of the town.

Walking back to the Old Quarter and the Djemaa el-Fna, we located the famous Café de France restaurant that Bryan had mentioned and that I had visited seventeen years previous, the self-same establishment that just about any travel writer who has ever visited Marrakech has sat at, had a drink and a smoke and jotted down their evocative thoughts and feelings. Compared to Bryan's description of the restaurant back in 1955, it appeared fairly unchanged in fifty years, and with the purchase of a cold drink, we too were allowed up onto the rooftop terrace that looked down over the square, to sit and gaze and jot down our most vibrant of thoughts. Looking to the south-east, out across and beyond the rooftops and minarets of this sprawling city, we could already see the High Atlas Mountains looming in the distance, the home of our sought-after Berber village.

View of the Djemaa el-Fna from the Café de France

The Djemaa el-Fna is an astonishing place. From our vantage point atop the Café de France, we could see how the stalls and sellers changed over the course of the day and night. Late morning, the stalls were initially divided into selling fresh orange juice and dried fruit, then later, a large group of barbecue people turned up in time for a lunchtime cook out. For the afternoon session, medicine men came on, selling cures for assorted ailments, often animatedly referring to a free-standing flipchart board they'd brought with them, showing the human body. Later, large groups of women started selling rows of identical baskets. There was also a shoeshine area and what appeared to be a garden centre section. Cyclists sped across the square, casting long shadows in the low springtime sun, and for the affluent tourist, horse-drawn carriages were available for a turn around the square. Just as I had witnessed in 1990, soon the white-robed snake charmers started to fill the air with their mesmeric, oboe-esque snake charming music, whose notes appeared to carry so effectively, even on a light breeze. Looking out from the roof terrace, the snakes still looked quite ropey (metaphorically speaking, though I suppose literally as well). Not far away, some blue-robed gents set up stall with a manky looking monkey sat on a box, ready to perform tricks for a fee. There were also finger cymbal players bearing their own special tasselled fez-type hats, who proceeded to wobble their heads to get the tassels to spin round. I couldn't work out if they were selling something or just performing. And walking amongst them for most of the day were the famous red-robed water sellers, hawking glasses of water, their wide brimmed hats and dangling tassels jostling gently in the afternoon breeze. And that was just during the daytime.

At dusk, out came the storytellers and performers, not dissimilar to the acts seen in Covent Garden in London's West End. Soon, the square was awash with teams of acrobats, all dressed in red, along with their accompanying drummers dressed in white, a small boy hoisted up to perch at the very top of their three-person living totem pole. From our vantage point on the roof terrace, we could sit and watch the entertainments unfold like some sort of wonderful Royal Variety Performance. But I felt a little detached – I needed to get down onto the square to see the sights and smell the smells up close. We paid up (really quite a cheap date as we had nursed those cold drinks for a couple of hours or so) and headed out.

Now in amongst what had grown into a heaving throng, we had to be careful – any inkling that you'd stopped to look or listen or indeed, got out a camera to take a photo, and you were immediately asked for cash. James and I tried to 'shoot from the hip'. This involved walking around with my camera strapped to my hand, pointing in the vague direction of the subject I wanted to capture and firing off a frame, hoping my camera's auto functions were working well. It's not that I was against paying for the privilege of taking a photo, but I was trying to capture a moment or two completely un-staged. The results were understandably a bit hit and miss.

As we wandered around, offers of hashish abounded, not overtly but cautiously, with sellers murmuring the word as they walked past us. To be honest, they walked past far too fast for us to respond quick enough, even if we did wish to make a purchase.

With the darkness of night enveloping the square, I found my senses quite overstimulated. Barbecue smells, burning incense, sweat, the rich scent of freshly squeezed orange juice as the sellers continued to sell their wares from stalls laden with vast quantities of fruit, the individual size of which you rarely see in the UK. We found the orange juice merchants to be very polite and smiley, more so than other sellers. The sounds of the square created an exotic cacophony. Noisy drums, tinkling hand bells, the snake charmers' flutes, all mixed together to form a dynamic soundtrack. The call to prayer then echoed across the square, broadcast from the city's many minarets, adding to the unique soundscape, which flexed and writhed as we walked around the square.

Djemaa el-Fna at night

8

Journey into the Mountains

While Bryan and some of the other team members relaxed on the roof terrace of the Café de France, Humphrey went bearing their letters of introduction, addressed to el Glaoui himself, to the palace of the Pasha of Marrakech. But bureaucracy was never going to be that easy:

Humphrey: We turned up at the gateway to the palace. There were a few guards who certainly didn't want to let us in and so this began one of these processes of endless waiting. In the end we waited long enough and was enough of a nuisance and eventually one of these guys carried in our piece of paper and then we got to see some young man who said alright, come back tomorrow. So it was our first introduction to the very different system of a tribal despotism if you like which was what el Glaoui was running at that time."

By 1955, T'hami el Glaoui held power over more than a million people and controlled most of southern Morocco. Along with his many titles, he came to be known as Le Grand Seigneur de l'Altas, effectively, the 'Sultan of the South'. His eldest son Brahim had control of the large Glaoui family kasbah at Telouet, which stood guard over the ancient caravan route from Marrakech to Timbuktu in the south. While the French supported the Pasha, they could convince themselves they still maintained a strong foothold in the governing of southern Morocco, but Glaoui maintained all the real power.

With a glance at the history books, it was no wonder Humphrey was having trouble getting an audience with any of the Glaoui family during those few days the team was stationed in Marrakech. During the month of July 1955, T'hami el Glaoui was having secret meetings with the French Resident General at his palace in Marrakech (the very same palace that Humphrey was stood outside hoping to gain entry and an audience with the Pasha). Glaoui had also sent one of his sons (Si Brahim) off to Paris to talk to the French Prime Minister. The French authorities had a plan that the puppet Sultan Aarafa would form a new representative government made up of members agreed by French ministers. But not only did Aarafa refuse to do this, the people chosen by the French to form the new government refused to stand. Also, Aarafa was now getting very keen to abdicate. Talks were at a standstill. On top of this, there were growing concerns that on 20th August, the anniversary of the exile of Sultan Mohammed V, the country would once again erupt into mass rioting.

Humphrey persisted, and after a lot of waiting around over a number of days, finally got an audience with another of the Pasha's son's Si Abd Sadek. He later wrote that the palace in Marrakech resembled a *Hollywood film director's idea of what should be the home of an eastern potentate*. The Pasha's son gave them yet more letters of introduction, particularly for the *Khalifa* (ruler) at the Glaoui's kasbah in Telouet, and supplied a *villainous-looking Berber* called Abdullah, who would accompany them and Humphrey noted, would go on to prove *very accomplished at intimidating uncooperative officials.*

Now bearing the correct permissions to continue into Glaoui's territory (plus a Berber escort), the team set off southeast, driving out of Marrakech, across a desert plateau and then started the steady climb up into the mountains of the High Atlas along the French-made road. Their destination was Taddert, around 100km away. The village consisted of a few stone built houses on either side of the road, with the sharp rise of the mountains forming a dramatic backdrop. This was to be their gateway to the Berber villages in the nearby mountain valley. Their first port of call was a bar/restaurant/hostel known as the Auberge des Noyers. Bryan wrote in his book:

The bar was a dark place. It had grimy painted walls, decorated with antique French adverts and even grimier marble topped tables… at the back was a small terrace shaded by almond trees.

The auberge catered for truck drivers supplying the French outposts in the south of the country. The patron had been in the foreign legion in the 1920s/30s and had seen the necessity for a 'halting place' on the road – he had built the inn when he retired from the army. When the students arrived, the auberge had a plaque displayed over its doorway revealing that it was a *Maison Recomandée* from the *1939 Guide Gatronomique International.* I looked into this guide but couldn't find much about it. Clearly, it was not quite up to the standard of the *Michelin Guide*, but still, some sort of pre-war French culinary recommendation all the same.

It was at the auberge that the team arranged to meet with

the local Sheik. A quick note: don't get too hung up on all these different titles (*Sheik, Khalifa, Caid* etc.). They all had (and to some extent still have) very specific meanings as honorifics or job descriptions within the Berber communities of the High Atlas, but as I understand it, these titles all generally mean 'leader' in some respect (over varying numbers of people or geographical jurisdictions). The meeting with the Sheik followed a typical course of proceedings. Bryan noted:

> *As is often the habit in Morocco a great deal of time was occupied with mutual introductions. We discovered not only that the Sheik was well and happy, but also that his wives and children were similarly blessed. We heard that his crops in the village this year were expected to be large. It is probable that none of this was true, but good manners demanded that it be said.*

The local French officials wanted the students to stay in Taddert and work close to the village, but Bryan explained to the Sheik that his group wanted to study the tribespeople in their own environment and not in the artificial circumstances of a halting place on the main road. He was concerned that Taddert was too influenced by outside forces:

> *A picturesque place, but many of its inhabitants had forsaken their traditional ways to ape the behaviour of Europeans.*

While negotiations with the local officials continued, the team set up camp in the garden of the auberge. Bryan recalled:

> *It was a pleasant place with a magnificent view across the valley to a small village on the opposite slopes. We sat out*

in the evening eating our supper under a trellised vine, watching the moon rise above the peaks and discussing our plans for the next few days.

The team wanted to find a suitable village located deep in the mountains well away (and isolated) from the main road. With only mule trails permitting access, the team decided to leave the truck at the auberge and explore the region on foot.

Humphrey: "We set out at first light. I can't remember how long the walk took us but we went this way and that and finally we came over what was obviously a pass and we came in sight of a valley. To me it was a Shangri-La, that sort of impression as if we'd come across a lost world. And we could see four villages. It was a very arid valley so the only colour was the green of the narrow terraces alongside the river all the way up. The rest was shale and dry. They had no wood to make houses and very little mud – these were very small little hovels made of stone. We came down and it was like a guardian angel view. People were out in their fields and they were calling out – we heard songs echoing from side to side of the valley. It was very beautiful. We walked on down the path, round a corner but then when we came out much lower down the valley, it was completely empty. Everyone had disappeared presumably taking refuge in their houses. So we sat down, and we very patiently waited. Eventually the heads of the women popped out above the houses. We later discovered that the villagers always put their women in sight first – they later told us that if a fight happened between villages, they don't hurt the women. They'd sent the women to spy on us believing we would not hurt them. They didn't know if we had hostile intentions or what it was all about and so at this point, we asked our guide from the area to go ahead and explain who we were and explain that we did have an introduction from el Glaoui."

Humphrey later wrote of how he was struck by the sheer isolation of the villages. They may have only been a few hours walk from the main road, but the students felt like they were stepping back centuries, to a land that time forgot.

The group was finally led to a village high up the valley, which they discovered was called Titoula.

Humphrey: "We were taken through these funny little houses and we came then into a big room where all the big men of the village were assembled around the edge. We sat down and went through all the courtesies. We had mint tea and eventually they asked 'who are you and why are you here'? So I did my best to explain through our interpreter that we were from England, we were students of Oxford University and if they would permit us we would like to study the animals and the plants and their agriculture. And would they permit us to stay in their village to do this kind of thing. This conversation went on a long time. They told us they'd never seen an Englishman before."

As well as Titoula, the team visited a number of the small villages dotted throughout the valley. At one called Tafraoute, the villagers were very wary of foreigners. At another, named Tamgruengenut, they were again not very welcome. The view of Abdullah, the Berber 'liaison officer' supplied by the Glaoui family was that all the people living in the valley were villains. It was back to Taddert to regroup.

Sat out on the shady terrace of the auberge, the students had an unexpected encounter:

Bryan: "This man came in and we couldn't figure out who he was at first. He spoke excruciatingly bad French and demanded a drink. He had a sort of equine face. He could have been an Arab. I decided he was Scandinavian. Peter was doubtful. He was sunburnt, but he was dressed in a sports jacket and then he had these very strange white shoes (which we later found out came from Iraq) and we were discussing audibly in English, you know I wonder what nationality he is and where did the white shoes came from, and he then turned round and said, 'Are you the people from Oxford?'"

That man was explorer Wilfred Thesiger. Born in June 1910 in Addis Ababa, Ethiopia, Thesiger was the son of the British Consul General and grandson of Frederic Viscount Chelmsford, a future Viceroy of India. He went to school at Eton, then on to study History at Magdalen College, Oxford (Bryan's college). While at Oxford, he was the treasurer of the Exploration Club and was awarded a university boxing Blue four years on the run. In 1930, he received a personal invitation from Emperor Haile Selassie of Ethiopia to attend his coronation and then in 1933, was back again in Ethiopia exploring the course of the Awash River. During World War II, he joined the Sudan Defence Force, helping to organise the Abyssinian resistance against the Italians and was even awarded the Distinguished Service Order.

After the war, Thesiger famously travelled across the Empty Quarter of Arabia and through southern Iraq, with further expeditions through Kurdistan, Pakistan and Kenya. He would go on to write many travel books documenting his expeditions and donated his huge collection of photographs to the Pitt Rivers Museum in Oxford. He was knighted in 1995 and it was Sir Wilfred that I had the pleasure of meeting while attending a talk he gave at the Exploration Club when I was at Oxford. He was a veritable God of exploration. But I digress. Back in the auberge at Taddert, in walked Thesiger…

> Bryan: "He had studied at Magdalen College in Oxford and I'm sure he'd heard that we were coming, presumably through the embassy or the Geographical Society or whatever. I'm not sure they didn't send him just to keep an eye on us to make sure we were not being stupid, like some sort of unofficial chaperone."

Bryan collected on a bet he'd had with the other members of the group that they'd meet at least one Oxford man in Morocco. This chance encounter with one of the world's most famous explorers came in very useful for the team when they needed to negotiate goods and services from the locals:

> Bryan: "Thesiger was quite an asset because he spoke Arabic fluently although he would bitterly complain that the people in Morocco didn't know how to speak Arabic properly. Anyway, he could talk to them and he impressed them because he always behaved as if there was a troop of cavalry following on just behind him over the horizon. He was with us one time when we were bringing in supplies on a mule train and he got fed up of riding the mules so he got off and walked. He turned round and looked and saw all the mule men were still on their mules and he went down the line pulling them off. 'If I walk, everybody walks'. And we thought what a rude fellow. The mule men later asked us if Thesiger was

a "Pasha" in our country, meaning was he some sort of man of authority. He knew how to behave and how to survive and he had been in a lot of places where it was very remarkable that he survived at all. We were always trying to be nice to everybody and then they thought that we were weak and in some ways we probably were, but he misbehaved in what seemed to us an entirely arrogant fashion with the locals. Although I was irritated with him at the time and thinking he was a nasty man, in retrospect he was demonstrating qualities that in his travels had probably saved his life."

Thesiger had actually come to Taddert with the intention of walking across the spine of the High Atlas Mountains to the town of Azrou in eastern Morocco, a journey of over three hundred miles. He convinced Bryan to let him take one of the team, Colin Pennycuick, with him for company. On 4th August, the two set off, with Thesiger carrying just a small suitcase. Colin would be gone for almost a month as he and Thesiger walked, rode and hitch-hiked their way across the mountains.

Now reduced to four members, the team still needed to find a suitable Berber village to study and so continued to explore the nearby mountain valley away from the main road. With input from the local Sheik, one village soon emerged as the front runner as a potential study site, where the villagers at least appeared friendly. That village was called Idirh.

With access to the village only by narrow mule tracks, the team would not be able to drive their truck into the valley and so Bryan now had to arrange to move all their equipment and supplies from their temporary base camp in the grounds of the auberge at Taddert to the village itself. Aided by their letter from el Glaoui's son Si Abd Sadek, a team of mules were provided by the local *khalifa*, but the mules themselves were a particular source of discomfort. Bryan later wrote:

> *The Moroccan saddle consists of a very thickly woven blanket which is thrown over the animals back and secured with strings under its belly. The front part of the blanket has pockets at each corner which accommodates the rider's toes and serve as stirrups. The Berbers on the whole are short men, and I found that when my feet were in the stirrups my knees projected above the animal's back. It was a very uncomfortable mode of transport.*

Loading their Moet & Chandon packing cases (packed with all their equipment and supplies) into the mules' panniers (again, great forward thinking with a dash of decadent elegance to boot), the mule trains set off into the mountains.

The trek took them over a high mountain pass and then down into the valley itself. Before them, wide, terraced fields could be seen stretching out all along the valley floor, cut into the land either side of a river. As before when they were scouting locations, in the distance they spotted men working out in the fields, but as they approached, everyone disappeared, with only a few women seen peeking out from the odd rooftop, keeping a wary eye on the group like some sort of meerkat sentinels.

After a five-hour trek, they finally arrived at Idirh. From first impressions, it struck them how the dwellings appeared to be expertly well-built, constructed mostly from shaped limestone rocks, with some having a mud brick upper storey. Each building was topped with a thick, thatched roof and was also joined to the next house in some fashion (e.g. via a shared first or second storey), creating a chaotically tessellated continuous structure, probably as a defensive feature.

Stone-built houses of Idirh ©Humphrey Beckett OUESM 1955

The students decided it would be best to set up their camp just outside the village, down near the river. Having erected their tents and arranged their supplies, it wasn't long before curiosity got the better of some of the villagers:

> Bryan: "They came down and chatted and we gave them tea and then others would come down. After they realised that we weren't after their kief or, you know, part of the law coming to descend on them, then they began to open up."

Their first visitors were three gentlemen each named Mohammed. One boasted he had ten mules (Mohammed Ben Ahmed), the second said he had one mule (Mohammed Bin Hameed) and the last said he had no mules at all (Mohammed Ben Ali). These men were dressed in traditional woollen Berber cloaks and generally wore some sort of turban on their heads, either of white or dark cotton. On their feet, they walked in open-toed leather sandals. Bryan was initially unclear as to whether they were offering their services (and their mules) or just announcing their 'mule worth' by way of status. These men appeared to be the village vanguard, sent to size up the Englishmen and get an idea of their intentions, but they did it in a friendly way with wide smiles. The village was already living up to its friendly reputation. Some of the village's young boys were also quick to come and see the new visitors, again dressed like the men, but instead of turbans, most wore white skullcaps.

One man, Lhassen Ben Idirh, cheerfully said that he would bring them fresh bread each day. Bryan was grateful, but it took a while to get used to this Berber bread:

The first villagers to the students' camp, Mohammed
Ben Ali and Lhassen Ben Idirh © OUESM 1955

His wife baked in her open-air oven. Dung was much used as fuel and since the dough was placed directly upon the fire, our daily bread often had unpleasant accretions.

While the students were 'worldly' men (as I previously mentioned, on account of their National Service), they were still very much accustomed to being looked after (remember their college 'Scouts'?). To this end, they sought a local person to come and help cook and clean at the camp. Bryan recalled in his book:

Mohammed Ten Mules was one of the first applicants for the job. When he came down to discuss it, we asked him about his health. He said he had been recently unwell and had journeyed down to the French doctor forty miles to the south. He proudly showed me the card which the doctor had given him. He clearly did not realise that it showed him to be suffering from tuberculosis. I felt it unwise to run the risk of employing him to prepare our food.

Spreading the net further afield, they visited the Sheik of the area who lived in a nearby village called Anammer, located near the top of the valley, and told him of their need for domestic help. A few days later, they were informed that a suitable candidate had been found: a young boy aged about seventeen called Brahim. Brahim was brought down to the camp and a wage agreed with the promise that he was a hard worker and a fluent French speaker.

He was one of the noisiest young men I have ever met. We discovered that his 'fluent French' consisted of about six words, but he could make a very satisfactory imitation of a motor car, a performance which he gave on every possible occasion.

Bryan wrote in his diary:

Brahim, our boy, is a menace – he talks a good deal too much and you never get any peace unless you keep him working.

Despite Brahim's oral annoyances, he became a valued member of the team, employed to fetch and carry, cook and clean and run various errands. With their camp now set up under a walnut tree by the stream that ran down through the valley, Bryan and his team started their studies.

Back L to R: Bryan, Colin, M'Barek, Brahim, Humphrey, Mohammed Bin Hameed. Front: John, Peter. © Humphrey Beckett OUESM 1955

9

The Berber Village

Leaving the hotel in Marrakech, James and I now began our own voyage of discovery into the High Atlas. Unlike when Bryan set out to the mountains, we knew the name of the village we wanted to get to and had forked out for a local Berber guide to take us there. But I was still slightly concerned from the conversations I'd had with the travel company that our appointed guide wouldn't know exactly which village was Idirh. Still, he could always ask for directions.

Our hotel had been perfectly adequate for our stay in Marrakech, despite the fact the shower was set at a scalding temperature. On the morning of our departure, out on the Djemaa el-Fna, the crowds and chaos of the night before had disappeared, allowing early rising tourists to wander around with their cameras and tripods and click away to their hearts' content without getting hassled for payment. It was clear that Moroccans (or at least those living in Marrakech) didn't do mornings very well.

As arranged, we were met by a driver who walked us out to his Land Rover, and we set off east in the direction of the Atlas

Mountains. En route, I noticed a fair few Toyota Land Cruisers and Land Rovers taking tourist groups off on what I imagined would be action-packed days out or camping trips in the mountains and rocky deserts. Along the way, the greens of the palmeries surrounding Marrakech soon gave way to ochres and reds of a more rocky, barren desert landscape. Just as Bryan and his team had done fifty years earlier, we pulled into the village of Taddert.

The village wasn't the prettiest I'd seen by a long shot, but it was instantly recognisable from the photographs the team had taken in 1955. While the outline or silhouette of many of the houses seemed to be completely unchanged, many of the buildings had been 'modernised' since 1955, with plaster now covering what was originally exposed brickwork, along with a lick of paint and assorted material awnings now stretching out into the road to provide shade. It had the feel of an American Wild West town, with buildings dotted either side of the road, and the mountain escarpment rising up steeply behind. Unlike when the students arrived during the summer months, when we drove in (in springtime) the high mountaintops in the distance were still capped with snow. On the day we arrived in Taddert, it was bustling with motor activity, much of which comprised of those Land Cruisers taking tourists on excursions into the mountains.

Just as the university students did decades before, and travellers had been doing for the past five decades since, we walked into the Auberge des Noyers for some refreshment. From the outside, the establishment appeared unchanged from the time the students first walked in, almost frozen in time. It still had a circular sign above its door, but we noticed it wasn't the *Guide Gastonomique International* plaque that had adorned the entrance back in 1955 – I caught sight of that now sitting over the bar inside.

We were greeted by Hussein, the current auberge owner, who showed us out to the terrace where Bryan and the team had had their first meetings with the local Sheik. The terrace was shaded by olive trees and overlooked a green and quite pleasant-looking valley stretching out below, exactly as Bryan had described it fifty years ago. It even looked like they had the same tables and chairs. Here, we met our Berber guide Talib, who reassured us he was very familiar with the area, yet in the same breath mentioned that he wasn't quite sure which of the villages up in the mountains was Idirh, but he would find out on the way. I wasn't overly filled with confidence, but you know, *insha'Allah*.

I'd had an idea that if we showed the locals some of the original photos taken by the team (which I had scanned at home and made copies to bring with me), then maybe someone might remember something, or recall something an elderly relative may have said about a group of Englishmen living in the mountains some fifty years ago. Our arrival at the auberge had already gathered a little group of men who were talking to our guide, so I got out the photos and asked Talib to ask if anyone recognised anyone. Soon our old photos attracted quite a bit of attention and we became surrounded by a whole gang of elderly gentlemen all trying to have a close look at the images.

Given the interest, I wanted to see if we could start trying to put some names to the faces in the old photos, so with my dodgy French and the aid of our Berber guide acting as translator, we told the story of the 1955 expedition. One man, by the name of Abdul, said (via our Berber guide, who translated) that he was from Titoula, the very first village that the Oxford team looked at when trying to choose their study site. Another old man with no teeth said he remembered the group of English students. We asked if Abdul or any of his friends that had collected round us recognised any of the people in the photos. One gent piped up, saying he recognised one of the photos as a chap called Ali Shishou (more about him and his family later).

It was exciting to arrive in Taddert, to sit in the time-frozen auberge, where the university students had thrashed out the

Excitement outside the Auberge des Noyers, Taddert

nuts and bolts of their expedition, and to meet some of the locals who were already helping us put names to faces and connect with the past. But we had come to find the Berber village of Idirh, and so we gently wrapped up the photo show outside the auberge, saying it was time to leave and head off, up into the mountains. Just as Bryan and his team had done in 1955, the plan was to walk in following the mule path that we'd been told was the only access route to the mountain valley, with our kit carried by a mule. Saying our farewells to the little group, our guide led us back down the main tarmac road to collect said mule and mule man, who rather surprisingly was there ready and waiting, his stable conveniently located at the start of the mule path. Looking onwards up into the mountains, we loaded up and set off.

I was bemused to note that the dirt path we started to follow was actually a fairly wide track as far as mule paths go. Then, I noticed some tyre marks. The mule man said (via our guide/interpreter) that around six years ago (in 2001), the old mule path into the valley was widened and this 'road' was built – it transpired that now you could in fact *drive* into the valley. Sure enough, we were soon passed by a large minibus crammed with people. But the road/track was rather precarious in places, cut as it was into the side of some steep rock faces, so I was rather glad we were on foot.

The air wasn't 'thin' as such, but it certainly felt Alpine, that wonderfully clean air you get atop European ski resorts on a crisp winter's day. Fortunately, we weren't burdened by our luggage and so, while the ascent was steep, it wasn't too hard going. The sky was that piercingly blue blue, not a cloud in sight. The terrain stretching out in front of us was mostly brown. In the mid-ground, some striking rocky geological strata now jutted out from the valley walls, and in the distance was the High Atlas, capped by snow.

As we walked further into the valley, around us the mountain peaks were continuing to rise up. In front of us, according to my map, was the peak of Djebel Tistouit, reaching almost 3000m at its summit. FYI: *Djebel* just means 'mountain', so every peak in the area is Djebel such-and-such.

Following the dirt road onwards and forever upwards, we reached a ridge and stopped for lunch. In front and beneath us, we caught our first sight of a string of villages nestled in the mountain valley. They appeared as small clumps of stone-built houses, sitting in an almost treeless and barren rocky landscape, with a strip of green hugging a river running down the valley.

Continuing onwards, the path now descended steeply into the valley itself. Around yet another bend, I spotted a narrow

The track leading us into the valley, with Djebel Tistouit in the distance

path going off to the right. Our guide informed us that this was the remains of the old mule track that led directly to the village of Idirh, but now it was 'broken'. I didn't quite understand how a path could be broken but accepted there was going to be a fair amount of discourse lost in translation, so we continued to follow the wide dirt track road as it snaked down into the valley. We could now make out that the swathe of bright green colour we'd seen from the pass was a vast and elaborate set of interconnected terraced fields cut into the otherwise barren valley floor. Some of the views before us looked instantly recognisable from a few of the students' 1955 photographs. By holding a photo out at arm's length, it was almost possible to line up the view, using the unchanged rock strata poking out of the valley walls as marker points. It felt quite special that we were potentially standing where Humphrey or Bryan had taken their photos of the valley fifty years earlier.

Ever onwards, the track turned down to a village we discovered was called Irhir. It was here we saw our first Berber villagers: young boys, mostly dressed in western clothes (trousers, hoodies and check shirts), who ran out to see who we were. The village girls mostly stayed away. The children who had collected around us looked to be aged from around four to ten years old, were generally very smiley, happy-looking souls, who were fine with having their photo taken (in fact, some requested it). Our guide was having all sorts of conversations with the children – I got the feeling that while he may have been imbued with 'local knowledge', he was (as we expected) quietly finding out which of the villages was Idirh.

Having walked down into the valley from our entry point over the ridge to the west, we then started to climb back up as according to our guide, the village of Idirh was situated much higher up the valley. Passing though the village of Taffraout, an elderly man came out to walk with us, so I showed him the old photographs. He thought he remembered the students, but not much more.

After five hours of walking (we had adopted a relatively slow speed on account of the thin mountain air and the often steep gradient), our guide triumphantly announced we had arrived at Idirh. We had found Bryan's Berber village.

The news that we had old photographs appeared to have spread like wildfire and the villagers were not shy about asking to see them. Even before we entered the village proper, we found a large, flat rock and laid out some of the old photos for the scrum of villagers (all male) to come and see. Great debate ensued as to who was who in each photograph, where a certain picture was taken, whose house was featured and even what houses still stood in the village. The Berbers of this area clearly loved photos. I noted that while some still wore turbans (as the old photos showed from 1955), many now wore skullcaps or were, in fact, bare-headed.

While I was excited by the immediate interest the villagers were showing in our visit, I was still a little anxious as to where

The villagers of Idirh looking at the photos from 1955

we might be sleeping that night. As part of the arrangement with the tour company, I had asked if they could help organise for us to be accommodated somewhere in the village itself. While we did have sleeping bags with us, we had not brought tents, so even though we could have slept out, I assumed at this time of year (March) it would get fairly chilly in the mountains. The tour company had said finding us a host would be fine (insha'Allah) but gave no further details.

Fortunately, there was nothing to worry about, as we were soon introduced to our host, a lovely man called Sharouk Mohammed Bin Saeed. I have a strong suspicion that negotiations for our stay (by our guide) all happened the moment we arrived (and not a second sooner) while the villagers were having a look at the old photos, but at least we now had a place to sleep the night. Sharouk led us through the village to his house and straight in for tea.

Our host's house was built of stone, with a thick plaster finish and had two levels, including a large, ground-floor storeroom and a walled courtyard. A few steps led up from street level to a smallish, red, metal front door, which opened onto a stone staircase, leading straight up to the second storey. At the top of the stairs, we were led left into a communal room. To the right was the kitchen area. We were then introduced to our host's three youngest sons: Khalid (age three), Mustafa (seven) and Saeed (eight or nine). Sharouk also explained (via our interpreter) that he had two much older sons, Rhashid and Hussein, who were currently away from the village, and two young daughters, Aisha and Fatima.

The communal room had whitewashed plaster on the walls and a large mat covering the floor, which itself was then covered with blankets (our boots were left at the threshold). The walls were adorned with a simple red diamond motif running around the top and a circle with a five-pointed star painted at one end. A single large window with small glass panes, set in a wooden frame, allowed the sunlight to illuminate the room, and at one end, there were two small TVs and a DVD player. When we were walking into the valley, I had noticed a chain of huge electricity pylons. According to Bryan, back in 1955 there were 'one or two' pylons present, but they just brought electricity over the mountain from Marrakech straight to the town of Ouarzazate in the south-east, and at that time there was no electricity supply to the villages. We were told by our host that only two years previous (2005), the villages were at last hooked up to the mains grid. As well as powering the villagers' personal entertainment systems, they now had electric lights in each house, and we would later discover that each village also had electric street lighting.

As was the custom, before anything, it was time for tea. A large, round, silver platter was brought out, as was a large kettle of water and a silver teapot, plus a set of glasses – always scalding hot tea in glasses, never cups. The kettle was heated by a portable butane gas burner and a protracted session of tea

Our host Sharouk preparing mint tea

preparation and tea drinking ensued, more of which I will talk about later.

Having partaken in all the correct 'first contact' procedures, we excused ourselves and went out for a quick walk to get a sense of the lie of the land of the village.

Unlike our host's home, many of the other dwellings in the village were not finished off with exterior plaster but just had the exposed rock masonry. Just as the university students had seen decades earlier, I instantly noticed that the individual buildings were tessellated with each other, joined either by the lower or upper-storey rooms, and one navigated around the village on narrow, unfinished (dirt) alleys. Most dwellings had a few cows and goats living in an adjacent walled courtyard, with an area of cover provided under the house. The flat roofs of the houses mostly had some degree of thatching on top but nowhere near as thick as we'd seen in the photos from 1955, with many now appearing to have just a layer of soil to keep the weather out.

Just outside the village, another impromptu gathering of menfolk rapidly surrounded us, eager to once again scrutinise the photographs taken in 1955. By this point, I was getting a bit confused as to who was who, and the confusion was spreading – our guide looked at me and started speaking in Berber as if I could understand him. He soon realised his mistake and then in English asked on behalf of the villagers what I planned to do with the photos. I could see where this was going and promised to give all the old photos to the village when we left – after all, they were not originals, just copies I had printed at home.

We were then corralled into another house (not unlike our host's) where we were invited to sit and have tea (again). Given the nature of the looks and gesticulations, I assumed we were the focus of a rather animated discussion, with talks lasting for some extended amount of time, but we obviously couldn't understand a word of anything anyone said, and our guide was too busy talking to the assembled men to provide any useful translation or explanation. Soon enough, the conversation ended with the arrival of a tagine luncheon of goat meat and couscous and everyone tucked in.

Now that we had located Idirh, Bryan's Berber Village, I was eager to learn about the village and its occupants, to see if we could identify the people in the photos and possibly even meet some descendants and discover how the village had changed and developed or indeed stayed the same over the last fifty years, but that would all come with time *insha'Allah*.

10

At Home in the Village

Back when Bryan was submitting his revised expedition proposal to the Oxford University Exploration Club, he put forward a wide and multifaceted plan of study, from the straightforward collection of native animals and plants and the geographical mapping of the village itself, to more challenging enterprises, like trying to understand the villagers' agricultural resource management, not least, what was grown, how much and how it was irrigated. Now they had a Berber village and villagers to study, the team set to work, albeit with one of their number (Colin) absent, as he was still off accompanying Wilfred Thesiger in his walk across the High Atlas Mountains. Humphrey later recalled that despite the fact they were all able students, they had no real idea how to carry out the proposed aims of their expedition. He noted:

None of us had done any fieldwork before. We were all very green.

Peter Galloway at the students' base camp ©Humphrey Beckett OUESM 1955

The four-man team split up, with each member concentrating on his own specialty. Bryan collected animals, Peter started to draw out a map of the village, John collected plants and Humphrey started to try and unpick how each of the villagers shared the available water to irrigate their own individual crops. Bryan was particularly interested in collecting insects and other invertebrates, and once the village children were aware of his interest, they often brought him specimens, such as venomous scorpions, in small cloth bags. He was also keen to collect some larger specimens and had a shotgun for such a purpose, which apparently was how they did it in those days. He wrote:

I had however neglected to ask the manufacturers to reduce the charge of the explosive, and the first time I went hunting, seeing a lizard on a rock about five yards away, I took careful aim and fired. The lizard disintegrated completely.

On another occasion, he came across an eagle sitting in a tree:

I fired. A single feather fell from the eagle's tail. The bird turned its head, gave me a withering glance and flew ponderously away.

The team soon acquired a few pets, including a pigeon, a ground squirrel and a chameleon. Writing home, Bryan kept his mother up to date with their growing menagerie:

Until a few days ago we had a chameleon called George who was a pleasant creature if a little bad tempered. Unfortunately, he departed when we were not looking.

However, before long, Bryan discovered his role as expedition zoologist was about to become Bryan Clarke, 'Medicine Man'. One day, not long after they had arrived, a Berber man came down to see them from the nearby village of Anammer. He said that his daughter had been scalded and now had a fever. Could Bryan help treat the girl? The nearest doctor was a Frenchman located some forty miles away and so, given that the team had their own (limited) medical supplies should any of them need treating, Bryan reluctantly agreed to tend to the girl's infected scalds and gave her some penicillin.

I had never given [an injection] before and I was extremely nervous, since a hypodermic syringe can be a dangerous instrument in the hands of the uninitiated. I was terrified.

Fortunately, Bryan's abilities as an (unqualified) medical practitioner proved to be successful. Three days later, the girl was cured. From that point on, Bryan was heralded wherever he went with calls of 'the Doctor is coming'. But given his unqualified status, Bryan was always cautious.

Although untrained as a medic, Bryan kept detailed patient notes on all the people he treated during his time in the village. Over the coming weeks, he attended to assorted swollen body parts, a wide variety of stomach aches and infections, fevers, scabs on the breast and headaches. I read with some interest in amongst Bryan's medical records that one poor chap came to him with painful testicles:

> *Sometimes the testicle swells and then he has pains in the stomach. He says he has had this for eight years.*

Sadly, there is no note as to how Bryan treated this specific case.

Many villagers came bearing pains in their joints, known as *Imuslmen*, thought to be caused by djinn (evil spirits). The accepted Berber treatment was to impale the patient with red hot needles, which were supposed to make the djinn uncomfortable and so the evil spirit would hastily depart, freeing the person from the pain. Bryan found that a dose of Epsom salts had a similar effect.

Bryan learnt about all sorts of local remedies, from burnt animal horns used for treating boils and scabs, to the consumption of assorted snails for coughs, corns and even typhoid fever. Penicillin and Codeine were the main curatives he was able to offer from the expedition's supplies. In a letter to his mother, he wrote:

> *It is very difficult sorting out the genuine cases from the spurious ones and we have not really got enough medicines… the serious cases we send to the French doctor but I don't suppose they ever get there.*

One such case was the sixteen-year-old wife of one of the villagers who was too weak and ill to walk. Bryan insisted she was taken to the French doctor immediately, but nothing he could say would convince the husband to make the journey. He wrote in his diary:

> His attitude was not born out of enmity towards his wife. Such a reluctance to visit the town for treatment was widespread. It was partly fear of destroying the beneficent effects of a saint's Baraka [spiritual power], partly for fear of her being sent to hospital and separated from friends and family.

Such was the anti-hospital sentiment that one day, a man came to see Bryan bearing a gunshot wound to the stomach, which he had received during one of the riots that had erupted in Marrakech. The man explained that he had walked out of the city's hospital, caught a bus, then walked across the mountains to the village. Fortunately, he survived and was still very much alive when the students left the valley.

As far as public relations were concerned, helping cure the villagers' ills was worth its weight in gold.

> It had the effect of breaking down the barriers of reserve between the villagers and ourselves, and it earned me my first invitation to dinner.

Treating ailments was one thing, but certain facets of everyday life, such as eating with the Berber villagers, involved a bit of training and considerable skill. Bryan later recalled in his book:

> Custom allowed us to eat with only the first three fingers of the right hand. There is a Moorish saying: 'To eat with one finger is a sign of hatred (and I might add, considerable

dexterity). To eat with two shows pride. To eat with three accords with the Sunna (the practise of the Prophet), to eat with four or five is a sign of gluttony'. We all soon fell into the last category.

As with most meals, the students found themselves eating copious amounts of mutton with couscous, which involved extreme agility. Bryan noted:

In the eating of kus kus, little balls are formed by a peculiar motion of the half-closed hand. These are then raised to the edge of the fist and dexterously shot into the mouth by the thumb. To do this properly demands considerable practise, and we succeeded in spreading a good deal over the carpet.

Along with eating the food, Bryan and his team had to get used to drinking significant volumes of sweet mint tea.

Mint tea is the Moroccan national drink, consumed in great quantities at every possible occasion. Preparing is both a ritual and an art.

Bryan: "It's quite a rigmarole to put in the mint leaves then the tea, pouring the hot water on it and then pouring off that hot water and pouring some more, then stuffing it full of sugar and mint and then pouring some more hot water on it and then letting it brew the right amount of time. It seemed to me that to make the best mint tea you had to get rid of the first pouring of tea and then it's the second lot of stuff which makes it particularly good. Then when you drink it, you make a lovely sucking sound otherwise it burns your tongue and then you are sitting there and going 'slurp', appreciating this tea and it's very refreshing."

The team quickly settled into the gentle rhythms of village life. Bryan wrote to his mother:

> I have to keep reminding myself that we are intrepid explorers because the tenor of life here is so even and timeless that one feels at home, much more so than in France or Spain.

In the evenings, they were often joined at their campsite by some of the important men of the village.

> Humphrey: "In Berber villages, of an evening the men like to gather just outside the village under a tree and they smoke and they chat and they gossip and so on. Well one of the places that they found it quite appealing to do just that was down at our camp, so we found of an evening we'd have Mohammed Bin Hameed and this person and that person and we'd sit down and gossip. Our interpreter was very good, you didn't have to say, 'tell him this and that', he would just immediately translate what you said, so you could get quite a fluent conversation going. And much of the conversation was really mildly obscene, you know, the sort of thing that men sort of chat about women and all that sort of stuff. So, we just sat down there and smoked and we gave them coffee or if they turned up earlier they might get dinner and so that's how it all started and we slowly built up a small nucleus of friendly people."

Now that the team was established, they were well provided for with villagers bringing them various foods. They realised very quickly that the key was to hit it off with the local Sheik or head man. In a letter home to his mother, Bryan wrote that he felt:

It is as if we have been transported back into the Middle Ages. The organisation of the valley is completely feudal. If the Sheik tells a man to bake bread for us, he does. If he tells him to give us his mule and his own services as a guide, he does so.

Being an earnest type, Bryan was worried they were being *provided for at the expense of the villagers who can ill afford it*, but at least he was offering his clinic and medicines free of charge by way of recompense.

Humphrey had also started his ethnographical studies, which to begin with were simple observations of daily life. He noted how it was left to the women to fetch the water for each household, often heaving large earthenware water jars back and forth to the stream. The women and girls would also milk the cows and fetch firewood for cooking, plus reeds from the stream to use as animal fodder. Out in the fields, it was men's work to keep the irrigation ditches free from blockage, along with ploughing, employing a single ox or a pair of mules to pull the plough.

As well as the minutiae of village life, Humphrey was also taking stock of the bigger picture, the sense of isolation within the valley and what that meant to the Berbers themselves. He later wrote:

At present, the people of this community are dependent upon their own resources. Having few contacts either economic or social with other communities, their life is confined to their own narrow valley.

Another of Humphrey's early observations was the apparent wide genetic stock that he saw in the faces around him. He wrote, *there are skins of every shade* and put this ethnic mixture down to *mass movement produced by poverty and wars in the past.*

Berber children ©Bryan Clarke OUESM 1955

***

Now that James and I had a place to stay in the village and had already been welcomed into a number of different homes, we continued with our exploration of Idirh. We wandered down to the river to try to find the place the students had set up their base camp. Sadly, it looked like the specific location of their camp (and the walnut tree under which they set up their tents) had been washed away. In fact, it appeared that the whole bend in the river had changed its routing, possibly due to a flood or two.

Wandering around, we also came across what appeared to be an old threshing circle – essentially an area of hard ground with a post in the middle to tie up whatever beast of burden they were using to help thresh their wheat. Threshing is the process by which the edible part of the grain is loosened from the straw, something that the hooves of a donkey or mule are well designed for. The circle looked unused but then we were in the village at the wrong time of year for any sort of active threshing activity.

Invites of hospitality were now coming from a number of directions and we found ourselves welcomed into the house of the village *Moqaddem* (head man), whose name was Hamid. We were told that the *Moqaddem* was a position chosen by the village members, an elected 'chairman' if you like, filled by someone who (it was explained to me via our interpreter) could 'get things done and get things organised'. His house was quite similar to those we had already seen, but I noted that he had energy-saving light bulbs – clearly a forward thinker. While in Hamid's house (drinking tea), the local Sheriff dropped in and invited us to provide our passport details. He joked that it was just in case we caused any trouble. It was also Hamid that provided us with dinner that night: a massive tagine of couscous and mutton. Wary of what Bryan had said about eating, James and I were concerned about our own dexterity to eat with the three fingers of our right hand, but our worries were unfounded. Everyone was provided with a spoon and tucked into the communal platter, along with three more rounds of tea.

Having had mint tea in other parts of Morocco during my travels back in 1990, I found this specific version to be quite different. In fact, on first tasting, I was not sure it was mint tea at all, but something more akin to green tea. But actually, the tea part of it was almost inconsequential – I witnessed the *Moqaddem* put seven large cones of sugar in each teapot. It was essentially hot sugar water more than anything else.

We were joined at dinner by a man called Brahim Bin Mohammed, who introduced himself as the son of Mohammed Bin Hameed (who Bryan had nicknamed 'Mohammed One Mule' on account of the fact he boasted he had one mule). This

Electric streetlights in Idirh

was quite a special moment as it was our first direct personal connection back to 1955. Brahim was very keen to see the photos of his dad. He told us that his father had died fourteen years ago and that he still lived in what was the family house and that we must come round for tea.

After dinner, it was back to our host's house. Just a few years previous, the walk through the narrow village alleyways would have been lit solely by moonlight or by a handheld kerosene lamp, but now, thanks to the arrival of mains electricity, our route was illuminated by a number of powerful streetlights.

That evening, our host Sharouk proudly informed us that should we need one, his house had a toilet. It was located halfway up the stairs leading to the upper storey and accessed through a small door, very much like the small door John Cusack used to get into John Malkovich's mind in the film *Being John Malkovich*. You had to bend over to step through the half door and only then, once in the toilet room itself, could you stand upright. The toilet was quite basic: a hole in the ground with no flushing mechanism and no paper. But as we later discovered, having a toilet (albeit just a hole in the ground) was pretty special in the mountains. For the majority of other villagers, to go to the toilet they simply took themselves out onto the hillside.

The presence of such a rarity as a toilet in one's own home gave us a strong hint that our host was clearly a significant and potentially wealthy member of the Berber village community. We later discovered that while the living apartments of his house were up on the second storey, it was in the ground-floor storerooms that his wealth was revealed in all its spectacularly explosive glory. As well as a well-stocked grain store, which I assumed would be commonplace in most of the villagers' houses, he also showed us his large store of butane gas cylinders. Back in 1955, most of the household cooking (and the boiling of water for tea) was done by lighting a small brazier using wood and charcoal. Nowadays, each household used a portable butane gas-powered burner, except when making bread, which was still traditionally baked using firewood (and dried dung) in an exterior bread oven. Given the size of his gas store, I could only conclude that our host was the main supplier of butane to the entire village. I might add that I was slightly concerned that we were sleeping above such a potentially explosive storeroom.

After a bit of television, we could barely keep our eyes open and indicated it was time for us to sleep. It was immediately apparent that there was no need for our sleeping bags as we were provided with many thick blankets to both sleep on and sleep under. The blankets were laid out in Sharouk's main room and then James, Sharouk, Khalid (the youngest son) and I settled in to sleep, all very toasty and warm. Little did we know that the following morning, our project to learn more about the Berber village and fully connect with the 1955 expedition, would be thrown into jeopardy.

Our host with the village's supply of butane gas,
stored directly under our sleeping quarters

11

A Run-in with the Authorities

Our first night's sleep in the Berber village was actually rather sweaty under all those thick blankets. With the sound of countless cockerels, we awoke fairly early the following morning. Breakfast was bread and olive oil, but I wrote in my diary that the oil tasted a bit weird, having additional notes of citron and coffee. Over breakfast, James mentioned that he thought our Berber guide Talib was being a bit offhandish following yesterday's meeting with the *Moqaddem*, and then more so after we were introduced to the Sheriff, who had requested to see our passports. It turned out that James's hunch was right.

Aware of James's thoughts on our guide's sudden change in behaviour, I started talking to him about this and that. It transpired that he was not actually an official registered guide and just a friend of the tour company's local contact, a man by the name of Allo Bassoo. Also, while chatting with him, I got the impression that our guide may even have had a previous run-in with the law and was possibly even wanted for some misdemeanour. He revealed that during all that chatting with the Sheriff and the

Moqaddem the previous day, he was warned that the Sheriff would report our unusual activities (e.g. showing old photographs) to some higher authorities. The possession of the photos and asking about the 1955 expedition was now troubling our guide. He then announced he felt he could no longer be our guide but just be an 'acquaintance', yet the authorities already knew he *was* our guide, so it all became a bit of a circular discussion.

This obviously all came totally out of the blue and so I was understandably getting a bit annoyed with him. After all, we had paid for his services and without access to the villagers and the ability to talk to them and to be able to take photos of people and try to explore the connections with the 1955 expedition, the whole raison d'être for the trip would amount to nothing. I was also getting a bit annoyed by his less than average ability to translate as well as I'd hoped.

Given the rumblings that were now emerging, even our host Sharouk said that we should possibly move off today and find somewhere else to sleep, perhaps in the village of Titoula, which is where the Sheriff resided. Overnight, it seemed we had turned from two people of interest to whom everyone was keen to talk to and see our old photos from the 1955 expedition, to some sort of super spies or ne'er-do-wells. With much toing and froing on the part of the guide, who was effectively trying to disown us, we decided that the person who could resolve this was the man who provided the guide in the first place, one Mr Allo Bassoo. James and I went out for a walk, now accompanied by our host's son Saeed, plus our guide, with the intention of making a phone call to Mr Bassoo to find a resolution. Given the prevalence of mobile phone masts attached to the electricity pylons that were dotted down the valley, this was, in 2007, eminently possible.

Leaving our guide to phone Mr Bassoo and fill him in on developments, we followed Saeed down through the village and out across the terraced wheat fields to the far side of the valley. I decided that if the whole thing was about to come tumbling down, I would make use of the walk to take photographs of the village so that we could at least try to make some sort of structural or organisational comparisons with what Bryan and his team had seen in 1955. We crossed the river, which I later discovered was called Tensift, and headed up the valley on the opposite side to the village.

As before, we soon collected a little group of boys to accompany us, with one insisting he even carried my tripod. The boys' attire of jeans and T-shirts made a stark difference to what the boys wore in 1955, where they were photographed wearing the standard issue traditional full-length Berber cloaks over cotton shirts and three-quarter-length cotton trousers. Clearly, western fashions and textiles had woven their way into the fabric of Berber lives, but only for the young boys. As far as I could see, the women and girls, plus all the older men, were still dressed in traditional clothes. Much as I was keen to ask why it was *only* the young boys that wore western clothes, I could never find the right words that would then translate (and be translated back) to achieve a revealing answer.

The boys of the Berber village wearing western clothes,
while the girls were dressed in traditional attire

We continued to walk on and wandered across the surrounding terraced fields, which, back in 1955, Bryan discovered were at least partially devoted to the growing of cannabis plants. From what I could tell, the fields were currently all down to wheat or other cereal. I'm of the understanding that hashish is still widely grown in Morocco, but no longer, it seemed, in the village of Idirh. Maybe with the fall of el Glaoui, the illicit trade in this area had dried up. Given our current predicament, I thought it best not to ask when and how the village's trade in cannabis came to a close!

Away from the village, we traversed across what looked like a defunct aqueduct and then past a large tank, and was told (mostly through mime by one of the boys that accompanied us) that it was a swimming pool! Possibly dual purpose?

Returning from our walk, we once again met up with our guide. He had spoken to Mr Allo Bassoo, his boss, or friend or whoever he was, and we were to phone him direct. During the call, I made sure that Mr Bassoo knew how annoyed I was, bearing in mind I had explained the whole project to the tour operator and so felt that everyone in the supply chain should have been completely aware of our needs and requirements. Apparently, the kerfuffle had emerged as the Sheriff did not understand *why* we had come nor *why* we were doing the things we were doing, i.e. showing the old photos and trying to work out who was who and talking to the villagers about the 1950s, which of course was not the most peaceful or stable time in Moroccan history. Between us, Mr Bassoo and I came up with a little ruse that perhaps Bryan was my father and he had wanted me to return to the village to give the old photos as presents to the villagers?

Mr Bassoo assured me that everything else would now be smoothed over and that we shouldn't worry. We could go about our business, but he suggested not to go into too much detail as to why we were so interested in the people of Idirh. What could have been a catastrophe had (hopefully) been averted, but I was still annoyed.

***

Back in 1955, the team of students also encountered a degree of hostility and wariness at the beginning of their residency in the village, not least down to the changing political landscape and the growing anti-French sentiment but also through a degree of natural distrust. While the six or so villages located along the length of the valley were all relatively close to each other (possibly just a fifteen-minute walk between nearest neighbours), they all kept themselves to themselves.

> Bryan: "They are fearful of others. There was a place called Titoula and the people in Titoula said, 'You haven't been to Idirh? They'll cut your throat in the night, you shouldn't be there, they'll kill you'. And then you go back to Idirh and they say, 'You haven't been to Titoula, have you? They're all villains, you know'. There's a very strict territorial thing. I was in Titoula and had given this man's daughter or wife some medicines and he'd given us dinner. It was just me and he felt obliged to escort me back to Idirh. As he got further away from Titoula and nearer and nearer to Idirh, he became more and more agitated and then he stopped and said, 'Now I've got to go home' because that was the edge of his territory."

But any mistrust the villagers of Idirh initially held against Bryan and his team of plucky Oxford undergraduates was perhaps fully warranted.

The expedition team: L to R Peter Galloway, Bryan Clarke, John Newbould, Humphrey Beckett and Colin Pennycuick ©OUESM 1955

The expedition truck 'Tartarin' breaks down en route through Spain
©Colin Pennycuick OUESM 1955

Dinner on the terrace at the Auberge des Noyers, Taddert
©Colin Pennycuick OUESM 1955

Wilfred Thesiger (centre) sat with Bryan Clarke (left) and John Newbould (right) ©Colin Pennycuick OUESM 1955

Loading up the mules with supplies ©Colin Pennycuick OUESM 1955

Our first view of the valley

Our host and his
sons, L to R Saeed,
Sharouk, Khalid,
Mustafa

Idirh,
the Berber
Village

Connecting with the
past: Invited in
to drink tea and
show old photos

Eating only using three fingers
of the right hand

At the village shop

Connecting with the past: The wife of Mohammed ben Ali

Connecting with the past:

Time travel at Telouet:

2007 and 1955

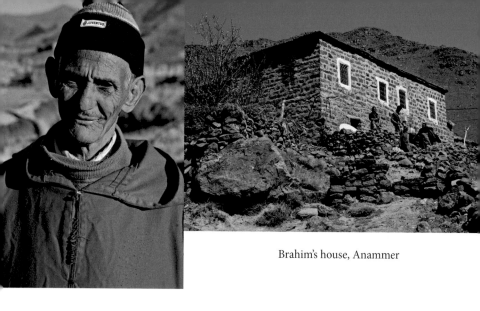

Brahim's house, Anammer

The students' domestic
help, Brahim

The author and James

Bryan Clarke
2007

Humphrey: "Put yourself in the position of these villagers. They were very isolated, no radio sets, nothing like that and they knew there was trouble brewing. They were el Glaoui's own people and were being called on to send men down to guard his palace in Marrakech. There was uncertainty – were the French going to be kicked out or not and if so, what happens to the tribes because they'd been supporters of el Glaoui and he'd been the supporter of the French? And then we turn up, these Europeans, these Christians. Some of our party wearing khaki trousers – we half looked like military. Were we French? Were we army? What were we about? Were we coming to spy on them? My role in all of this was dealing with that sort of issue, just spending time talking via our interpreter, physically calling on people and talking to them and just generally trying to say, well actually, we're not spies and we're nothing to do with the French."

Unlike our little hiccup – which was centred on the intricacies of us asking unusual requests and the fact we weren't behaving like more normal tourists who, on occasion, pass through the villages in the valley – in 1955, the country as a whole was teetering on the edge of a nationalist uprising against the French colonial rulers.

Humphrey: "As the situation got more and more dangerous for the French, Bryan was very worried that we were at risk with these people. I mean, if they had chosen to turn nasty we were completely helpless. And as I look back on it, I think our main defence was we didn't look French and we were so obviously naive and really non-streetwise that we couldn't have been a serious risk."

Beyond their secluded valley, the Nationalist movement in Morocco was gaining ever more traction. The country, particularly in the south, was facing a potential civil war. In the first few weeks of their stay in Idirh, Bryan wrote in his diary how he had talked to one of the villagers about el Glaoui and the power and influence he wielded. He noted that the local man believed that *the Glaoui are ready for war. They will fight with the French against the rest of Morocco.* But the tide appeared to be on the turn even from within Glaoui's supporters. A few weeks later, Bryan wrote again in his diary that a son of one of the villagers came down to their camp. He had been in the Pasha's guard in Marrakech.

> *He said he had joined the Pasha's Guard because he wanted to be a Mehazinya (policeman) but now that the Pasha is with the French, he does not want to be one. He did not like the French.*

These complaints by the Berbers against the French and el Glaoui were still mere whispers, private (and secret) thoughts shared among friends. Bryan wrote to his mother:

> *There is much complaint at the moment because the Pasha is arming them to act as police in Marrakech – they do not want this and are more interested in ploughing their fields and growing their hashish on which they make a pretty handsome profit.*

While the momentum of change was evidently building, the nationalist sentiment had now reached the Berber villages in this isolated valley in the High Atlas, with el Glaoui's loyal Berber tribesmen now starting to question his association with the French. As the students continued their studies in Idirh and beyond, they were unaware that change would soon engulf the entire country.

12

Life in the Berber Village

Settled into their camp (located next to the stream just outside the Berber village), the university team soon fell into a daily routine:

> Bryan: "We would get up in the morning soon after sunrise and eat a leisurely breakfast. Peter would then set off with plane table, compasses and clinometers to draw his map. Humphrey would make his way to the village, John would depart into the surrounding hills to collect his plants. I would remain in camp to deal with the dozen or more patients that appeared every morning."

Bryan wrote in his diary how the village's menfolk were rather theatrical in their suffering:

> *Never were there so many men with headaches gathered in one party. Some of the acting was magnificent. Men wailing, clutching their heads, looking deathly pale. Many had obviously missed their vocation in life.*

A page from Bryan's personal diary

Bryan found himself treating all sorts of maladies, from TB and dysentery, to boils, syphilis, rheumatism and many different types of injuries. When people came seeking treatment, they would often bring a gift, such as a chicken. Bryan's bush clinic was so popular, he started to run low on medical supplies, but from a receipt I found from a company called The British Drug House Ltd, it appeared that he was able to secure a restock of medicines, which were then flown out to them.

The four students soon gained their own unique reputations in the village: Humphrey for curiosity, as he asked so many questions about village life; Bryan for his medical abilities; John for his poor sense of direction; and Peter for his strength and silence. The villagers were now so used to the Englishmen, that offers of companionship were put to the students. A 'go between' offered the team the opportunity to arrange liaisons with any of the village women they desired, for the princely sum of 250 Francs. The offer even included married women. Bryan later wrote in his book:

> *I do not know what would have been the feelings of husbands about such arrangements. We did not consider it discreet to inquire.*

Each evening, the four men would write up their day's notes and diaries by the light of a paraffin lamp, with the added bonus that the lamp would also attract a stream of insects, which were then added to their growing zoological collection.

> *We could see the whole valley spread out below us, and as the sun set, it glowed with the intense colours of evening. We could see little figures returning to the village from their day's work. Snatches of song drifted up on the evening air. With darkness, small lights appeared all over the valley.*

As part of their studies into the Berbers' way of life, the team were also interested in understanding the physical structure and makeup of the village. Peter drew a detailed map, revealing a total of twenty houses, with up to ten people living in each dwelling. Recalling in his book the design and structure of the houses of the Berber village, Bryan wrote:

> *I use the word 'house' for want of a better one, but these bore in fact a closer resemblance to maisonettes. The first floor of one family's dwelling was quite often above the ground floor belonging to another.*

The average Berber house was quite a humble affair:

The room was not whitewashed. The mud plaster flaked from the walls, the single window had no glass. A dirty mule pack was heaped in one corner and a threadbare carpet covered half the floor. There was no other furniture.

Bryan also discovered that not all homes in the village were the same:

The house demonstrated the opulence of its owner in having a large square window which was protected by a complicated wrought iron grid, and which even contained a plate of glass. The expenditure of money on putting in windows was what the sociologists would call 'conspicuous consumption'. Rich Americans have Cadillacs, rich Berbers have windows.

***

Fifty years later and by comparing the expedition's photographs and Peter's hand-drawn map of the village with what we could see in front of us, James and I found that, structurally at least, much of the village had remained unchanged in the intervening decades. We identified many of the houses noted in 1955 as still standing, presumably passed down through the generations. There was some evidence the village had grown, but you could see that all the houses (old and new) were built to last, made of carefully cut chunks of solid rock, with floors supported by thick, wooden beams and no evidence of the infiltration of poor-quality modern build materials. But there were many other significant changes, not least the provision of mains electricity for electric lights and the advance of modern technology by way

Our host's cosy living room/bedroom

of mobile phones, satellite TV and DVD players, plus the butane gas burners now used for cooking. The homes we were invited into were all warm, comfortable and clean.

As I mentioned earlier, our host's house occupied two storeys, with the ground floor made up of the toilet room, the living space for the livestock and the two large storerooms, both secured by large wrought iron doors and hefty padlocks. Up the stairs were two rooms, one either side of the top of the stairway. To the left was the living room (which contained the televisions) and was the room in which we slept, along with Sharouk and one or two of his sons, at least while we were present in the house – maybe his wife and daughters also slept in there under more normal conditions. Other than a low, wooden table brought out to serve food on and used in the preparation of tea, there was no furniture as such, just floor coverings and blankets. The second room contained the kitchen and the area where (while we were present) Sharouk's wife and his daughters slept. The house also had access to a roof space.

We were invited into enough other houses (for tea or some sort of meal) to appreciate they all had a very similar arrangement to our host's home. Many had exactly the same complement of items: the low wooden table, a full set of tea-making equipment and maybe a television. The prevalence of small, glass windowpanes held in place by wooden frames in all the villagers' homes suggested that glass was no longer restricted to the rich but now available to all. Electric lights were also prevalent, but electric plug sockets hadn't yet been plumbed into the walls, and dangerous-looking cables and extension leads brought power into the living rooms.

In 1955, the village had one shop, run by the *Moqaddem*. It sold sugar, tea, coffee, dates and something called carbide? I've looked up 'carbide' and all I can find out is that it is a chemical compound containing carbon (still none the wiser). An old friend of mine informed me that back in the day (I did say he was old), you would add water to the carbide to create acetylene gas which would power carbide lamps. By all accounts, Bryan saw the shop as quite a small retail enterprise:

> *It was only a minute hovel of a room with a counter made of tea chests, but it faced the open space at the centre of the village.*

Despite its small size, the village shop (much like village shops all over the world) was the place to catch up on all the town gossip, i.e. who was getting married, the latest prices and any news from out of town picked up at the weekly souk in Taddert or Telouet.

When we visited Idirh, we discovered that commerce within the village had expanded by a full one hundred per cent as there were now two shops. One (with a red door) matched the description of the shop Bryan described, located on the town's small square, but when we rocked up, it now sold such western luxuries as wellington boots, Panten Pro V hair shampoo, some sort of Daz washing powder, sweets and of course, tea and sugar. This was run by a man named Abdullah. However, there was also a second shop (with a blue door) run by the current *Moqaddem* (Hamid), who sold very similar things. Both shops were restocked once a month with a delivery now driven in from Taddert in the back of a van – far easier than the mule trains of the past.

Life in the village was generally centred around meals. Meals were always a shared experience, either with the whole (and extended) family or other members of the village. Breakfast was a sort of porridge. Lunch and dinner were invariably a tagine of couscous with either chicken or mutton, plus bread and the weird tasting olive oil. Once we had got over the issue of being allowed to go about our business and stay in the village, we were once again of interest to the villagers and were continually invited into people's houses for food, whether we had just eaten or not. Our experience of Berber food was that it tasted pretty good, most of the time, and there was a lot of it. Yet, I didn't see any overweight or obese village members and so could only conclude that the calorific intake and the physicality of life in the mountains were in balance.

***

Bryan's own recollections of some of the dishes he ate in the village were not always that fond:

> Bryan: "You would be walking in the mountains and the shepherds would say come and eat. You couldn't say no (well we didn't know how to anyway) and they would produce this maize porridge with sour milk and rancid

butter and black things of uncertain origin floating in it, perfectly disgusting. You knew you had to eat it and you knew that when you ate it, the next day you would get the trots. And that was an inconvenience."

Along with taking detailed observations of the general way of life and customs of the Berber people living in Idirh, part of the team's ethnographical study was to investigate how it organised itself on a day-to-day basis. It was the team's historian Humphrey who took the lead. He discovered that it was in the 1930s (only twenty years previous) that the villages in the valley had gone through a significant change:

Humphrey: "The valley was the highest valley before you crossed over the main watershed of the High Atlas Mountains along the old trade route from Marrakech to Ouarzazate, down the River Draa and across the Sahara to West Africa. That had been an active trade route until the time of the French Protectorate and the establishment of a motor route well to the west of this traditional trade route. So while they were on the trade route, the villagers' main source of income derived from the caravans that were passing through the village."

The valley was originally part of the great caravan route leading from Marrakech to the south. Caravanners would lodge in the villages en route to the likes of Timbuktu – maybe this was why hosting travellers (like us) was not seen as anything out of the ordinary, as it dated back to a centuries-old tradition. While the team was camped in Idirh, one of the elderly villagers, by the name of Si Hadj Lhassen, recounted to Humphrey how, before the French had built the road (which now ran from Marrakech to Taddert and off to the south), he had made his money running mules, taking salt and sugar to the south and then returning back with dates to sell to the north. But the building of the new road meant that trade now bypassed the Berber villages like Idirh, and so things had to change for the Berbers to survive.

> Humphrey: "It was only after the road was built that they needed to develop their agriculture to the extent that it was going when we were there. So the whole irrigation system had been built up relatively recently, perhaps only over two generations."

Large terraces had been cut into the rocky landscape either side of the river running down the valley in order to create fields to grow enough food to feed each village. Each 'field' was supplied by irrigation channels which took water from the river through a set of gates which could be opened and closed. These channels were still in place when James and I arrived. Back in 1955, Humphrey made it his job to investigate how the villagers decided whose fields were irrigated each day and for how long. On the face of it, it seemed overly complicated, but he soon discovered that all the arrangements were simply discussed and agreed at the village mosque. But growing crops in the dry and arid valley was not easy:

> Humphrey: "These people had a very hard way of life. They were surrounded by great beauty and I didn't have any sense that they warmed to the beauty of their surroundings. To them it was just the Autumn of reality, scratching a livelihood from a hostile place because really there was very little soil that high up the Atlas range."

On the question of what crops the villagers grew, there were the usual array of maize, barley, rye and millet, but it quickly became apparent to the students that the villagers were also growing cannabis plants to supply the illicit trade of hashish. In a letter home to his mother, Bryan explained:

> *Although it is forbidden by French law, the village of Idirh lives off the cultivation of hashish which is sold in the black market in Marrakech. The other day the khalifa sent his men round to collect taxes on the hashish. These taxes amount to a bribe to the khalifa to keep quiet about it.*

Humphrey calculated from the size of the fields that the village could grow enough food to feed all its inhabitants, with a bit of extra cash coming in from the sale of the hashish.

While we were there, we saw nothing but food crops growing out on the terraces. Admittedly, any hashish possibly wouldn't have been on public display, but we did do a lot of poking around yet found nothing. While we were staying in the village, there didn't appear to be much heavy work going on out in the fields, but it was March, so I assumed planting had already taken place (the cereal plants were already growing) and harvest was a fair way off. We often saw some of the village boys out on the scrubby land away from the green fields herding their goats. Given the barren nature of the valley away from the stream and the terraced fields, I would have thought the boys had to cover quite large distances to find enough food for their goats to eat.

While the valley may now boast mains electricity, mobile phone masts and satellite dishes, they didn't yet have running water in their homes and the only household mod cons were the butane powered portable gas cookers. As to the division of labour, particularly between the sexes, little appeared to have changed in fifty years. Just as Humphrey had found, in and around the house it was a case of a woman's work was never done. In Idirh, it was still the women and girls who collected the water and cooked all the meals, and it was the women and girls out washing clothes in the stream, laying them out on the banks to dry. As for the men, we discovered that it was their job to go to market, source various household or village supplies, work the fields, oversee the running of the village and of course, make the tea (the last of which took up a considerable amount of any man's day). Indeed, during the time we were staying in the village, most of the menfolk spent the greater part of each day sat around talking (or making tea).

One night, James and I were out walking when we heard singing drifting along on the night air. Following the sound, we came across a group of young girls standing under a street lamp, all singing with great gusto. The songs were often accompanied by a simple rhythm played on a drum that looked like an oversized tambourine. While we obviously couldn't understand the lyrics, the singing seemed to have a lot of 'call and answer' type phrases, where one group would 'call' and another would then 'answer', all in song, with the tempo increasing as the song went on.

A night-time singalong was another facet of village life that clearly hadn't changed in fifty years, and possibly had remained unchanged for centuries. Humphrey was privileged to witness both a song and dance:

Humphrey: "Once or twice in the village, in the evening, they had a dance and this was superb because there were about six drummers and the drumming was of a subtlety that I'd never previously encountered. I seem to remember it started with a group of young men and then, one by one, the girls insinuated themselves into this line. The women have a way of dancing in which they move flat-footed, it's not like European ballet where you go up on your tiptoes. They advance their foot in a way that is very sexually suggestive. With this wonderful music, the rhythms they were drumming out changed from one sort of beat to another and you suddenly realised that this was something different, but you couldn't see how it had got there from one to the next. And then they got into all sorts of spontaneous singing."

Bryan wrote to his mother, telling her that *the Berber singing is very strange indeed. It sounds most like early church music, ending each phrase on a high note.* He later wrote in his diary how the music *can create an atmosphere of mystery and unlikelihood.* I loved that turn of phrase, the notion of 'unlikelihood', very enigmatic.

***

With the run-in with the Sheriff forgotten and the issues with our guide now resolved, we were able to continue our investigation into all the various aspects of modern life in the Berber village, not least the making and drinking of Berber mint tea. My assumption that we had not necessarily been drinking *mint* tea was proved correct, as the tea for sale in the village shop *was* in fact *green* tea (as I had suspected). It was rather worryingly called Gunpowder brand, so named because the tea leaves are rolled into small balls and dried, giving them a resemblance to gunpowder. One day while we were at the shop, some of the village children came in to buy lollipops. Ripping out a sheet of paper from his notebook, James showed one of the boys how to make a paper airplane, something none of the boys had ever seen before. The resulting plane flew very well and then was the centre of a little fight to gain ownership, so James made a whole set so that everyone could have one. I wondered if our instructing this small group of kids in how to make paper planes would catch on (i.e. would they share their knowledge with other kids), and had we inadvertently changed something about the village by introducing this alien concept? For sci-fi fans, had we fallen foul of *Star Trek's* 'Prime Directive', whereby you are prohibited from interfering with the natural internal development of a civilisation? Given the villagers' recent access to hundreds of satellite TV channels beamed in from around the world, I doubted it.

We also discovered that, along with a small mosque, Idirh had its own hammam (bath house) for personal washing, but it was only big enough for two people to use at a time. With at least two to three hundred bodies living in the village, I wondered how (and when) they all washed. Again, just like the irrigation timetable, perhaps it was discussed and agreed at the mosque each week, but I wasn't going to upset our newly restored relationship with the villagers by asking such a personal question.

As well as my film and digital SLR cameras, I had also brought an old-style Polaroid camera that spat out instant prints. I didn't realise when I threw it into my camera bag back in England how useful it would be as a fabulous way to ingratiate ourselves with all the locals, as I could take their photo and give them the print straight away. As I said earlier, the Berbers of Idirh seemed to love photographs. Sitting in the shade outside the *Moqaddem's* house one day, some of the village elders started to line up, requesting to have their portrait taken. In exchange for an instant Polaroid portrait, the villagers were now more than happy to talk to us (via our guide) and to invite us into their homes, particularly those of whom that we had an old photo of their dad, uncle, cousin or mother, taken back in 1955.

One such man (who we'd met earlier) called Brahim, who was the son of 'Mohammed One Mule' (Mohammed Bin Hameed) came and found us and invited us into his house. As with all the Berber homes we'd visited, it comprised of one living room with a kitchen room located off that main room. His house or, more accurately, his apartment/maisonette, sat above his neighbour's ground-floor dwelling, locked together like pieces in a 3D game of Tetris. He had a picture of his dad on the wall and again, was keen to have his own photo taken. He made us tea, plus bread, and then brought out some walnuts, which he cracked open with a special double-headed nut hammer.

Soon, we were joined by a man who introduced himself as Omar Shishou – that surname now sounded familiar. He revealed he was the son of Ali Shishou, one of the men who had known the students back in 1955 whom we had already identified in one of the old photos, which fortunately I had with me and so presented to his son. We were then invited to Omar's house where he brought in milk, fresh from the cow, and offered us eggs cooked to perfection. It wasn't long before we were joined by his brother Hussein, who I remembered being one of the most excited chaps on that first day when we walked into the village and started showing the old photos. Hussein explained that he was the keeper of the village's electric flour milling machine and invited us to see it at work. For centuries (possibly millennia), flour was milled laboriously by hand, using small circular millstones. Now everyone in Idirh brought their grain to the Shishou brothers to be mechanically milled.

Later, as we walked back through the village, we were introduced to the wife of Mohammed Ben Ali (the man Bryan called 'Mohammed No Mules'). Mrs Ben Ali was one of the only women in Idirh who requested to have her photograph taken and of course, we obliged.

Word must have got out, as later on, our host Sharouk asked if we would take a portrait of his wife, too. While the instant Polaroid photos could be given out there and then, my main camera was my Digital SLR – using this, I could only show the villagers their portraits on the small view screen at the back of the camera. I promised I would get all my images printed and posted back to the village as a thank you for their generosity.

Sunset in the valley was, as expected, a visual riot of colour. Given the steep valley walls, you could watch the dark shadows racing up the rock face as the sun sank behind the mountains. I am always amazed at just how pretty sunsets and sunrises are in wild places. I assume it has something to do with the clarity of the light.

Soon after sunset, the myriad stars would come out, unobscured by any clouds or city haze, giving us a particularly clear view of Orion and his belt. In the distance, a group of young Berber girls started singing once again, stood as before under the bright yellow light of an electric street lamp. Back at our host's house, dinner was a massive tagine of rice with added fresh milk. The texture and consistency were such that, if I had added sugar, it could have been a rice pudding. Settling in for bed, for some unknown reason, James and I got the giggles. I'm sure our host thought we were quite strange. In the night, I heard one of Sharouk's young sons sleeptalking in Berber.

13

A Chance Encounter

One day while James and I were out exploring the valley, we had a chance encounter. As usual, we had collected a small posse of boys who were happy just tagging along. The children of our host were more confident with us than their friends and would insist on carrying our camera tripod as some sort of banner of privilege.

Walking back to the village, we were introduced to an elderly man we'd not seen before. He was revealed to be none other than Brahim, the 'domestic help' employed by the students back in 1955. Now, almost seventy years old, word had got to him up at his own village of Anammer and he had come down to meet us. We were bowled over. With a single handshake, we had made a direct connection back through time to someone who had played a significant role in the university expedition.

Fifty years ago, Bryan found the seventeen-year-old Brahim both useful and a distraction:

It was a relief to have somebody who would do the washing up. Brahim however was a mixed blessing. His six words of French and his imitations of motor cars became very tiring after we had heard them the first hundred times. He had boundless energy and great enthusiasm not the least of which concerned his love life... many of the villagers tended to be indiscrete in their amorous activities and we had trouble with a number of them who developed attachments to Brahim.

Unlike in 1955, when we met Brahim, his French was now very good and we could talk direct to each other *en français*. We chatted about the expedition and took photographs (I thought that Bryan and Humphrey would love to see what had become of their man servant). It transpired that Brahim was now a bit of a legend in the valley, a man of high reputation and quite revered, for what reason we couldn't immediately work out, but his age alone would have put him in good stead for elevated reverence. He was dressed in a traditional Berber cloak and woollen hat bearing the word 'Juventus', which he revealed was his favourite football team. We learnt that he'd run a shop in Taddert for some time and so was well connected both in and outside the valley. As it was getting late, Brahim had to bid us farewell to return to his own village, but he said we had to come and stay with him as his guest.

Brahim, the students' domestic help, came and found us

With this invitation to stay with Brahim in the nearby village of Anammer, our time in Idirh was now coming to a close. We gave our host (and his children) a set of presents we'd brought from the UK to thank him for his hospitality. At no point was I ever asked for any money to cover the costs of our stay, but it's possible this may have been covered by our guide.

As usual, we were up early to witness another glorious sunrise and for a chance to once again wander round the village, camera in hand. It really was a very beautiful place, cut off from the outside world by the looming mountains flanking both sides. I say 'cut off' but, now with a strong mobile phone signal and a smattering of satellite dishes, the villagers were only geographically isolated. But even the mountains were no longer much of a barrier – the widening of the mule path from Taddert to make a dirt track meant that if they had the financial resources, the villagers could now buy a car and drive in and out of their valley home should the urge take them.

Following breakfast, it was up out onto the roof terrace via a small door to clean our teeth – a morning activity that amused our host's children. I didn't see any evidence of a Berber toothbrush while we were staying in the village, but then that may have been a personal activity that was none of our business. I assumed the Berbers cleaned their teeth in some manner, as bathing their dentition in highly sugared tea every two minutes would surely mean they would be toothless by their teens, but in fact, most of the villagers seemed to have fairly good-looking teeth, even in older age.

Another round of family portraits were taken, with much handshaking and smiles, and we were on our way. While we were obviously saying goodbye to Idirh, we weren't 'leaving' the valley just yet, just expanding our research area.

It was a fairly short walk up the valley (with a bit of puffing and panting due to the thin air) to the village of Anammer, to the house of Brahim. A mule was arranged to take our luggage and the walk was very picturesque, allowing us to look back down along the whole length of the valley. Led by our guide, who seemed to know his way this time, we arrived at Anammer in about fifteen minutes and proceeded to walk almost to the top of the village to Brahim's residence. Even from the outside, the size and build quality of his house, which included ornate iron grills over his windows, reinforced my belief that Brahim was now a wealthy man. The house also boasted a large satellite dish which he said he'd installed the moment electricity arrived in the valley two years previous.

It turned out that our guide Talib was a friend of the family, somehow related to Brahim's wife. And talking of Brahim's wife, unlike in Idirh where we barely saw a female soul, she appeared to be on a much more 'equal footing' (for want of a better phrase) with her husband, in the sense that she (and their daughter) didn't hide away and were in fact very chatty with us right from the start.

Entering the house, the large communal room was similar to many others we had seen and Brahim was keen to explain how he had four different satellite receiving frequencies from the one dish, giving him two hundred channels per frequency (making a total of eight hundred television channels). He went on to show us his DVD player and a car tape player. Brahim also had a mobile phone, permanently stationed in the kitchen, which he explained was the best place in the house to get a strong signal. I was initially surprised that a phone landline had not been installed along with the electricity, but if you think about it, that is a whole lot of additional wires and telegraph posts etc., going to each house – with cellular mobile phones, you just need to put up a series of phone masts and the job's done.

Tea was provided with the usual elaborate ceremony. I couldn't be sure, but the teapot and large round tea tray both

Brahim invited us to stay at his house in Anammer

seemed to be made of solid silver. If so, these were incredibly expensive items and I assumed would have been ancient family heirlooms, passed down father to son.

It was at this point that James needed the toilet, but unlike Sharouk's house in Idirh, there was no toilet facility chez Brahim. It did slightly amuse me that he had every latest entertainment and communications technology but no toilet. As James's need increased, I recalled something Bryan told me about a certain phrase they used in the village:

> Bryan: "Having a crap, if you'll pardon the phrase, is called 'Paying the Blacksmith'. Now, I think there is some degree of prejudice here, because blacksmiths for some reason in the Atlas Mountains are almost invariably Jewish and I think that it was a ruderary about Jewish people."

Without a household toilet, you simply took yourself off to do your business (and 'Pay the Blacksmith') wherever you liked. Unsure of where to go and how far to go away, James was led off by Brahim's eldest son Abdhamen. But one question bothered me: with neither household nor communal toilets, how did the land deal with all the villagers crapping everywhere, for centuries? I suppose the valley was a big place, but I felt it far too impolite to question our host on this matter.

There was certainly a different vibe in Brahim's household compared to what we had experienced in Idirh. At lunchtime, we were even invited into Mrs Brahim's kitchen to see (and photograph) mother and daughter cooking. There was a lovely beam of sunlight coming through a hole in the roof which we bounced into the darkened areas (using my trusty photographic reflector) to take very naturalistic photographs. Boasting a wide assortment of pots and pans, cooking, as in Idirh, was conducted on a portable gas burner.

Brahim's daughter Zahra was also very keen to show us the household water pots, which were the traditional heavy earthenware type. These were incredibly heavy, so it's no wonder they now prefer to use the modern lightweight plastic jerrycans. Fortunately for the people (actually, just the women and girls) of Anammer, they didn't need to go all the way down to the stream, as they had a nearby well to draw up fresh water.

Lunch at Brahim's house was chicken and chips, fabulous gravy and salad. Afterwards, we brought out the remaining old photos to show to Brahim and his family. He fondly remembered the English students, telling us how he worked for them in a domestic role, washing up, fetching and carrying and, of course, translating for them with his *excellent* French. Mrs Brahim asked about my own family and so I dug out photos of number one and number two son – the photos soon got kissed.

An initial exploration of Anammer and its surroundings took

us further up the valley, where we discovered the village's huge wheat fields growing on terraces similar to every other village in the valley. Out away from the fields, unlike in Idirh, in Anammer it was the village *girls* who were out tending the small flocks of sheep and goats. Perhaps Anammer didn't have many young sons to put to work, or perhaps the village was more egalitarian, with women and girls involved in a wider array of jobs and subsequently taking on an even greater percentage of the work?

It was up here, wandering around the upper reaches of the valley, that we saw the most amazing geological strata (rock layers) projecting out from the valley walls. The Atlas Mountains are rather a complex geological construction composed of six separate regions, all built over several different geological time periods. We were currently standing in the High Atlas, a region sandwiched between the Anti Atlas of the south and the Middle Atlas to the north – the range continues all the way up through Algeria and into Tunisia. The mountains are predominately made of sedimentary rock, mostly layers of limestone, plus some sandstone thrown in, and it's down to the sedimentary rock that the Atlas range is famous for its wide abundance of fossils, which would have formed during the sedimentation process millions of years ago. Fossilised creatures such as ammonites and belemnites literally fall out of the valley walls, to be collected up and sold to passing tourists at any possible opportunity.

The clearly defined rock strata are so visible because the limestone layers are interspersed by chalky clays (called marls), the result of different geological processes occurring during the time the whole area was sitting at the bottom of the ancient Tethys Ocean, some sixty to two hundred million years ago. Due to the collision between the African and Eurasian tectonic plates, the rocky seafloor was forced up, creating the Atlas Mountains. Further tectonic activity then shifted and twisted the rocks, and that is why the rock layers are often seen angled in all manner of directions –

it's mostly down to the enthusiastic teachings of geologist Prof Iain Stewart, with whom I worked with on a number of BBC science shows, that I love geology and rocks so much.

Dinner at Brahim's was a well-attended event, with two other women and their children joining us. Mrs Brahim brought out freshly baked bread which had the texture of a pain au chocolat. With the arrival of dinner, the television was switched on. We watched *The Score*, starring Robert De Niro, with Arabic subtitles.

The exertions of the day, plus the high altitude, sent me and James off to sleep, for us to be woken around 9pm for the rest of dinner (couscous). Having taken a family portrait (Brahim, his wife and daughter and three sons), it was time for bed.

Striking rock layers near the village of Anammer

14

Au Revoir

The students lived in the Berber village for just over seven weeks. For much of that time, they found themselves cut off from the outside world, living in a rather isolated bubble. But beyond the village, and beyond the valley, tensions across Morocco were still rising.

> Humphrey: "I had to go across to Taddert for some reason and I was there as the morning radio broadcast came in and the news item was the massacre at Wassane. This was the biggest single incident in which a group of tribesmen descended on the French mining town of Wassane and wiped out the entire European French population. The only people that survived were a small number who got to the police station. The European Civilian Administrator went out with some police. I think they were mounted on horses, but they were wiped out. The people who came down from the hills went into the hospital and they not only killed the French doctor, they killed all the Moroccan nurses and all the Moroccan

patients and I think there was something like 120 people dead. It was against that background that we were living in the village and Bryan, who after all was responsible, thought it was getting tricky."

Bryan was particularly worried about the approaching date of 20th August. This was the anniversary of the deposition of Sultan Mohammed V Ben Youssef (who later returned from exile to become King Mohammed V of Morocco). He later recalled:

It was whispered that Morocco would rise against the French, that all Europeans would be massacred, that communications would be cut and that the country would declare independence.

The students knew one man from Idirh who had served in the Pasha's guard and he was not happy. He did not like the fact the Pasha (el Glaoui) supported the French. Bryan noted him saying *we are faithful to the Pasha because he is one of our tribe, but we cannot agree with his actions. If you had been French, we would have burnt your camp to the ground.*

Humphrey: "We were in the valley and it was the time when the tax inspector came out from Telouet. He would say to people, 'OK, you want to sell your cash crop so you pay me such-and-such'. They stoned him out of the village. So, there we were just over the hill from Telouet and el Glaoui had already lost his clout amongst his very own people, so we knew things had really changed. The men were coming back in droves from Marrakech. All the people who had been drafted there to try and keep Marrakech under control, they were just simply deserting. We knew it was breaking down."

The Berber men returning to the village from Marrakech, had been drafted by Glaoui to keep the city under control but now appeared to be deserting their posts. Even during the short time the students were living in the village, the Pasha's power seemed to be on the wane. But there was always the lingering question as to whether el Glaoui ever had *full* control over the Berber tribesmen of the High Atlas. In the wider sense, yes he did. He was Lord of the Atlas and, despite the wider presence of the French authorities, Glaoui was the de facto ruler of the Berber tribes of southern Morocco. But Berbers were known to be incredibly good at *self-regulation* for want of a better phrase. For centuries, the Berbers of the High Atlas had effectively governed themselves, both within each village and between the villages of the valley. Yes, they had to pay taxes to el Glaoui, but that was just a financial inconvenience – the Pasha didn't really 'govern' them as such. Humphrey later wrote how he believed the Berbers actually refused to allow any outside force to govern them. He continued:

> *Perhaps it is because they refuse to tolerate any regulation of their life that these Berbers have always remained in their isolated mountain communities.*

It's an interesting thought – did the isolation of the mountains confer on them this intolerance of outside control, or were the people themselves intolerant of exterior forces and so used the geography of the mountains to help act as a physical barrier?

With their time in the valley coming to an end, the students had made such a strong impression on the villagers, the Sheik tried to get them to stay, offering Bryan a house and a wife:

> *It was an appealing idea to stay in this isolated village, to live in reasonable comfort with one or two wives to*

do the hard work, to make a modest living treating the
inhabitants for their ailments and to forget the need for
gaining a degree and finding a job.

It was with a heavy heart that the group packed up their tent and supplies. Everything was loaded back into the Moet & Chandon champagne boxes, secured to a train of mules and, saying their goodbyes, they walked out of the valley. By now, it was becoming more evident that change was about to engulf the whole country. But putting aside impending political upheavals, the march of the modern world could also soon breach the valley walls and infiltrate the time-locked Berber village they had come to love. Bryan wrote:

A man could be peaceful and happy [here] but how long,
I wondered, would it last? How soon would western
civilisation itself come to the valley, improving the
material well-being of its people but not perhaps making
them happier or more content... A vague picture might
remain, but we would perhaps fail to recollect the vision
of evening shadows slanting across the valley or the sound
of shepherds singing on the mountain sides.

***

Our own departure from the valley was also now fast approaching. It began with a breakfast of semolina, which, to be honest, tasted like unsweetened gravel. We found that in the mornings, we were generally still quite full from the countless meals and after-meal meals that our new host Brahim had provided.

On the day of our departure, Zahra (Brahim's daughter) said she would bake us some fresh bread for the journey and insisted I come and see their bread oven in action. It was an orb shaped

Brahim's daughter Zahra baking bread in a traditional Berber oven

structure, fashioned out of hardened clay and earth, with a fire burning inside and a large hole through which you placed the bread dough, similar in some respects to an Indian tandoor. It pretty much matched an image Bryan had taken of a Berber bread oven fifty years earlier.

Our guide had rustled up a man and a mule to carry our bags, and we said our goodbyes to the family. Brahim insisted he walk with us for part of the way, then left us to go tend to his crops. He was a fascinating man – a man of some wealth, education and influence; a man who had gone places and made a name for himself. He was also a man who had embraced many new emerging technologies to create a twenty-first century version of what was essentially still a medieval Berber livelihood, located in the High Atlas of Morocco.

While we had originally walked into the valley from Taddert to the west, we were now walking south, up and out of the valley to the town of Telouet. Even though the village of Anammer was quite high up the valley, it was still a fairly long walk, passing

Electricity pylons built along the path of the original Great Caravan route

the Sheriff's village of Titoula, which didn't look as nice or welcoming as Anammer or Idirh.

It was exciting to realise that the path we were walking on was the original path of the Great Caravan route, which for centuries took trade from Marrakech to the Sahara and back again. Sadly, there were no camel trains bearing exotic goods, just us shuffling along. Unlike the road in from Taddert, this path had not been converted to a road for motor vehicles, so it still held much of its ancient charm. That is, if you ignored the large electricity pylons, which snaked all the way down the valley – I couldn't find the correct collective noun, but someone online suggested a 'hum' of pylons? We were told that these pylons were the ones put in by the French back in the 1950s, when the electricity was being carried down the valley and out the other side yet still effectively bypassing the villages. Brahim mentioned that in 2005, the cables were replaced with some sort of high-tension wires, and it was this that finally facilitated bringing electricity direct to the villages.

Continuing on, we started seeing lots of mineral crystals scattered across the rocky ground, particularly one with a shiny grey sheen that I recognised as gallium nitride, something widely used as a semiconductor in electronics. Clearly, there was not enough to mine, otherwise I imagine someone would have staked a claim.

Walking onwards, we passed odd bits of old trees here and there. Trees were very rare in the valley away from the river coursing down the middle, and we were told that it was these gnarly bits of wood (as opposed to the fruitful olive and walnut trees) that the women of the villages would seek out for use as firewood to power their traditional bread ovens. I was surprised there was enough salvageable wood to supply all the ovens in each of the villages down the valley but soon realised that perhaps the main fuel constituent used to bake the bread was still dried animal dung.

Eventually, we reached the very top of the valley. Pausing for a moment, we looked back to take in the complete view stretching off into the hazy distance, glowing in all its vast brown and red glory. Stepping over the rocky ridge, we left the valley and the Berber villages behind.

Walking down the other side, we were immediately buffeted by an icy wind. In the distance, a wide, flat plain stretched out as far as the eye could see. On the ground, I noticed lots of dung beetles (I can't help being a zoologist), one of which was even rolling a bolus of dung, taking it back to a subterranean nest for later consumption. Around us, the colours in the rocks were also changing from the yellows, browns and reds that were dominant in the valley, to more green, even bluish-coloured rocks. We soon discovered this colour change was restricted just to the steep slope we were currently scrambling down, as out in the distance, a dusty red hue was once again prevalent.

After a rather civilised packed lunch of bread (thank

you Zahra), Laughing Cow cheese, yoghurt and oranges, we continued down around a hill, passing a rather grubby-looking village, to arrive at the desert plain below. In the distance was our next centre of exploration and investigation: the town and former Glaoui stronghold of Telouet.

15

Time Travel at Telouet

Just as James and I did over fifty years later, the Oxford students walked out of the valley with their mules carrying their bags, up and over the pass and down to the village of Telouet. Here, they were greeted by the site of its imposing kasbah, which at that time was revered as the 'most beautiful castle in Morocco'. Bryan wrote in his book of *an impressive sight, lying as it does in the centre of a vast red dust bowl enclosed by bleak mountains.*

Telouet was one of the Glaoui family's most significant strongholds. According to Gavin Maxwell in his book *Lords of the Atlas*, it was:

> *Ill ordered, ill planned but majestic in its proliferation and complete absence of symmetry... a tower of tragedy that leaves no room for laughter.*

Bearing their letters of introduction, the students entered the kasbah through its massive wooden gates which led into a walled courtyard. Here, they were met by the *Khalifa* of Telouet.

Bryan later recalled:

We strolled through the courtyards of the kasbah, it was a scene straight from the Arabian Nights. In each courtyard there were carpeted ledges on which white-cowled figures greeted us solemnly as we passed by... women were driving cattle across it to an arched doorway on the other side, mules were being unloaded and the Khalifa's Vanguard was being backed into a rococo garage. Some of the Pasha's long-limbed lean Saluki hunting dogs lay panting in the sun.

Telouet sits at around 1800m elevation and occupied a strategic position in the High Atlas, located as it was on the old caravan trail and being close to a number of salt mines, including one that extracted the prized pink salt found along the Oued Mellah (Salt River). The building of the kasbah started in 1860 but was enlarged in the early 1900s. Legend has it that three hundred workers took over three years to decorate the ceilings and walls, often using ornate terracotta tiles covered with enamel in the form of chips set into plaster, known as *zelliges*. The students found the opulent nature of the fortress staggering, yet many eyewitness accounts, dating right up to the eventual fall of T'hami el Glaoui, tell of horrors deep beneath the richly decorated rooms – the dungeons of the kasbah were said to be filled with the enemies of the Glaoui family, left to rot away. Glaoui also had a habit of mounting severed heads on spikes adorning the ramparts in true medieval style, just as he did at his palace in Marrakech, but as Bryan never saw any, the Pasha may have let that practice slide by the 1950s.

The kasbah of Telouet ©Bryan Clarke OUESM 1955

When the students arrived, the white plaster adorning the exterior walls of the kasbah was gleaming in the bright summer sunshine. The kasbah's extensive garages were also filled with expensive motor vehicles, including the Vanguard Bryan mentioned, and luxurious rooms awaited them.

Bryan: "It was very atmospheric and, as the evening came, there were various people lying about on carpets on little terraces, smoking their kief and looking exotic, and then we were given a room to stay in. We had dinner brought in by what I would only describe as large Nubian servants. We had this dinner on silver plates – it was very posh, lolling about on the carpet and eating this exotic dinner. And then, in the morning, they came in with breakfast, which were rather nice Moroccan doughnuts and coffee with really hot pepper in them which would wake you up in the morning."

It was at the Telouet kasbah that the team were reunited with their fifth member Colin Pennycuick, who had returned from his walking expedition with Wilfred Thesiger. The group was now joined by yet more European explorer types, Ernest and Susan Gellner.

Ernest Gellner was a British Czech philosopher and social anthropologist. He had studied at Balliol College, Oxford and, at the time the students met him and his wife, he was working at the London School of Economics in the sociology department. The couple were out in Morocco researching (and I have to quote this as I'm not entirely sure what it means) 'conceptual critiques on the analysis of kinship to frameworks for understanding political order outside the state in tribal Morocco', a study that would go on to become his book *Saints of the Atlas*.

Having briefly reunited, the team soon decided to split up again to explore more parts of southern Morocco. John Newbould now joined Thesiger and they set off to climb Djebel Toubkal, the highest mountain in North Africa (4167m), a mountain I had climbed on the Exodus trip I went on back in 1990. I don't recall it being the hardest of climbs, more a steady, slow slog, but we did have to overnight on the way up at a little refuge building, so it certainly wasn't a quick climb. Setting off from the refuge at sunrise the following morning, I remember a scree path led us up to the summit. Coming down was much quicker than going up, and according to my diary, it only took a couple of hours to get all the way back to base camp. The speed of descent was aided by a bit of *scree jumping*, whereby you run down the steep scree slope, launching yourself into the air, and just as you land and slide on the loose rocks, you launch yourself off again. Something for the young (and young at heart) – I wouldn't do it nowadays for fear of twisting my ankle, but aged seventeen, I was fairly unbreakable.

Humphrey decided to head off with the Gellners to explore several towns and desert oases in the south. He was particularly interested in continuing the study he'd begun in Idirh, investigating traditional Berber pottery and pottery techniques – we'll rejoin him again later. Colin, Bryan and Peter planned to drive south to collect more animals.

***

When James and I arrived at Telouet, our guide led us to a guest house and then said his farewells. He hadn't been the best guide, but at least he had got us safely to Idirh, found us a wonderful host to accommodate us in the village and got us out the other side. After freshening up (and making good use of the fully functioning water closet toilet facilities), we were offered tea and realised we were now in the land of actual *mint* tea as opposed to the Gunpowder brand *green* tea served in the Berber villages. We immediately made a bee line to go and see Glaoui's famous kasbah of Telouet.

When Morocco gained its independence from France in 1956 (the year following the students' expedition) most of the Glaoui family (being French sympathisers) fled the country, leaving their lavish palaces and kasbahs unoccupied. For some reason, possibly on account of its very close connection with the ousted traitor, no one took up residence in their imposing kasbah at Telouet and it soon fell into disrepair. As well as being immediately ransacked back in the late 1950s (one would assume by Nationalist vandals) and then neglected, we discovered that in the 1990s, an earthquake had caused severe structural damage to the desert castle. What we were seeing was a ghost of its former self.

The kasbah still looked vast and felt very imposing, but from the outside, the ramparts were now brown/red in colour, not the gleaming white-plastered walls the students had seen. In places, great chunks of plaster were missing, revealing the mud bricks beneath. This former vision of an edifice in luminous white was long gone. Everywhere, the walls were crumbling with decay. Walking around the outside, we came across a group of boys playing football in what would have been a grand parade square.

Approaching the front entrance, the impressive studded wooden doors Bryan had walked through when they arrived were now hanging loose off their hinges. Walking through, we could instantly see where the team had taken some of their photos back in 1955. Holding the old images in front of us, it felt like we could time travel, using the photos as a conduit to jump back to the 1950s heyday when the students had been welcomed in – a time of opulence, of servants (slaves?), visiting dignitaries and a castle in full and luxuriant fettle.

Continuing our exploration around the outside of the kasbah, we found the garage where the Pasha had kept his fleet of cars, plus the stables, both now lying empty and decrepit, the whole place stained brown from the red dirt and flaking with decay.

Asking around, we were able to locate the Guardian of the kasbah who, for a small fee, agreed to let us look around inside the building itself. He told us his father had also been the Guardian before him and that the massive key he was using to unlock the doors would have been the same key used in 1955. Walking through to an inner courtyard (possibly the same one Bryan had described bedecked in thick carpets), all we could see was decay and disrepair, with broken balconies and even whole walls now lying as rubble.

We were then taken up some stairs into a large chamber and on through to a reception room. Our guide explained that this was where the members of the Glaoui family would have entertained guests. Within this room, we could at last start to see what the kasbah would have been like back when Bryan and his team were invited in and entertained here. Around us, the walls, floors and ceilings still bore richly tiled mosaics, elaborately carved architraves and pillars. The colour palette was mostly quite muted, with browns and reds, but some of the rooms also boasted blues and yellows, the tile work made up of highly intricate repeating square and circular patterns. Given the incredibly poor state of the outside of the building, I was amazed these rooms still looked so good, but I believe a degree of renovation had recently taken place. I couldn't quite understand the Guardian's explanation, but it was possible that surviving members of the Glaoui family had paid for some of the repairs.

Sumptuous reception hall inside the kasbah of Telouet

In one room, there was an ornate painted wooden ceiling and wooden window shutters. In another, there was what would have been a large, glass skylight illuminating the room with natural light. Sadly, now with the glass all broken, the room was left open to the elements. Huge, wooden doors were still in place, separating lavishly decorated rooms and chambers, and small fireplaces stood at the ends of each room. In what we thought was a main bedroom, pink and red silk panels bearing geometric patterns were still present on the walls. It wasn't difficult imagining the place coming to life, with people dressed in fine clothes, lounging on thick Berber rugs, the sound of chuckling water from a fountain in the courtyard, servants bringing round plates of food and drink, being served tea from bejewelled silver teapots, the sound of one of those snake charmers' oboes wafting through the air and, dare I say it, the intoxicating haze of hashish smoke adding to the otherworldly experience. OK, so I did go a bit *Arabian Nights*, but, you know, it probably wasn't that far off. The students must have had a splendid time spending the night as guests of the Glaoui family.

The Guardian then led us up to a roof terrace, with the various turrets still bearing many of the curved, brightly coloured, green-glazed roof tiles. Standing up there, we could see the true scale of destruction across the buildings that made up the kasbah, with crumbling walls, broken windows and tiles, rusting twisted metal that made up the broken skylights (which looked a lot like the carcasses of mini greenhouses) and a number of large storks now in residence, sitting in their even larger nests. This once revered fortress was now just a crumbling shell, albeit with a few preserved gems locked away deep inside, protected by a lone Guardian and his large, ancient key.

El Glaoui's kasbah of Telouet now in ruins

16

Discovery at Ouarzazate

After a short stay at the lavish kasbah of Telouet as guests of the Glaoui family, Bryan, Colin and Peter upped sticks and drove south in their truck *Tartarin*. Their first port of call was the desert town of Ouarzazate. Bryan wasn't overly impressed, writing in his book:

> *The town has two cafes, a military hospital and several barracks. It reminded me for some reason of a settlement in the early days of the American west.*

Ouarzazate had the nickname 'The Door of the Desert', and during the French occupation, it was considerably expanded as a garrison town, an admin centre and a customs post. It was in Ouarzazate that the students were joined by the sixth and final member of the expedition team, Charles Pasternak. As a postgraduate researcher, Charles couldn't spend the whole summer in Morocco as he was expected to work on his doctoral thesis during the long summer months. He'd arranged to come to Morocco for just a couple of weeks to conduct a separate side-project, investigating the biochemistry of Berber blood. The origins and genetic makeup of the Berbers of Morocco is a complex story, possibly including the Basques of the Pyrenees, the Semitic people of Arabia, plus wide genetic mixing with Arab peoples over centuries, and so Charles wanted to see if he could find any evidence of abnormal haemoglobin molecules (found in blood) that might be characteristic of these southern Berbers. For this, all he needed was some willing volunteers from whom he could take a pinprick of blood and run it though a simple, handheld, battery-powered paper electrophoresis machine.

When Charles arrived, he was able to bring news from the world outside the Berber village. Having caught the train down through France and Spain, Charles crossed into Morocco via Gibraltar and caught a bus to Marrakech. Here, he encountered the night-time curfew, actively enforced by French police carrying submachine guns. Continuing on to the kasbah at Telouet, he sought permission to conduct his project from Glaoui's *Khalifa*:

> Charles: "I remember going there... on my own with the interpreter and coming to this huge fort, made of mud bricks and somebody coming out and I proudly presented a piece of paper and said, 'I've come here to analyse blood samples and it's quite alright, I have permission from his Excellency el Glaoui'. The man looked at me rather suspiciously..."

Charles discovered that even here, at the heart of Glaoui's power, the Pasha's control and influence was on the wane, as despite having a letter of authority signed by the Glaoui family, he was told in no uncertain terms that he would need to gain permission from the French authorities, and that meant travelling north to seek an audience with the Ministry of Health in the country's capital of Rabat.

After a bit of toing and froing, fortunately permission was granted, but the Ministry didn't give Charles free range to pinprick Berbers willy-nilly. He would have to limit his study to a military hospital based in Ouarzazate. From Rabat, he began hitch-hiking back south again to rendezvous with the expedition team and start his project. On the journey, it became clear how quickly the French were losing control to ever more bloodthirsty nationalist gangs. Along the way, he was picked up by a French couple from the town of Oued Zem. They told Charles how their daughter and grandchildren had been killed in a sickening attack:

> *The town had been taken completely unprepared. People were murdered in their homes. A doctor was cut down among his patients in the hospital... The girl had been preparing to go out when a gang of men broke into the house, chopped off her head with a hatchet and killed her children. Her husband returned to find them all horribly mutilated.*

Oued Zem was a French settlement in the centre of Morocco. On 20th August 1955, the day of the anniversary of the exile of Sultan Mohammed Ben Youssef, Berber tribesmen marched on the town and set about a frenzied slaughter of the European inhabitants. Patients were even massacred in their hospital beds. Seventy-seven people were killed, brutally hacked to death. Charles also reported that in Marrakech, the medina was now surrounded by French troops. All the phone lines had been cut and, outside of the city, el Glaoui followers were deserting their posts, with nationalists gaining further control. The French hold on Morocco was clearly slipping away.

In amongst all this terror, mayhem and bloodshed, Charles still felt he had a job to do. The doctor at the hospital in Ouarzazate allowed him access to any Berber patients who were happy to spare a drop of blood. Even as a postgraduate student, Charles was at the cutting edge of biochemical research:

> Charles: "The technique for separating abnormal haemoglobins from normal ones was just being developed at that time and because people were finding interesting things about abnormal haemoglobins in different races of the world, particularly the Mediterranean, I thought it might make a nice project to try and see what kind of haemoglobins the Berbers have as opposed to the rest of the population. So I set out to do just that."

When Charles later returned to Oxford, one of his professors was rather blunt about the political situation in Morocco:

> Charles: "He said, 'Well, Pasternak I don't know why you had to take needles, you might just as well have taken a bucket! So much blood flowing there over the last six weeks whilst you have been away.'"

***

Our own journey to Ouarzazate was far less terrifying than Charles's (no massacres or bloodshed), but nonetheless, quite frustrating, as most travel plans can be in Morocco. The idea had been that our guide would get us as far as Telouet (which he had done), and then he would arrange a car to drive us down to Ouarzazate. But, as with most timed arrangements in Morocco, a deadline was only kept *insha'Allah*, that is, if God wills it. We waited some hours for our ride, only to be told by the brother of Mr Ala Bassoo (Mr Bassoo being the local travel agent person we'd contacted while in the Berber village when our plans had hit a stumbling block) that the man they had arranged to take us could no longer take us and that we were to take a taxi. Hours later, our taxi finally turned up, and off we went, only to stop five minutes outside Telouet. Unable to communicate effectively with our taxi driver, we had no idea what was going on. Half an hour later, three elderly ladies came out of nowhere, got in, and we set off (again).

To put it bluntly, Ouarzazate was not the prettiest or most interesting of places in Morocco. It had the feel of a 'stopping off point', a chance to refuel, refresh and then get going to wherever you actually wanted to go to. Our hotel was once again a rather modest affair (Hotel Amlal) but perfectly suited for our needs (bed, shower, toilet). Heading out into the town, our first stop was the Kasbah Taourirt, arguably the only real site of historical interest in what was otherwise a rather dull and dusty town. As you might expect, this was another Glaoui palace/fortress, but apparently, neither he nor his upper echelon chiefs ever took up residence and it became a home for his second-tier commanders.

Built in the nineteenth century, it had almost three hundred rooms, and while the kasbah was partly ruined, it had now undergone some restoration work funded by UNESCO. I noted that the building had many tiny doors (for what purpose?) and elaborate interconnected rooms, and so wandering around, James and I got quite lost. The walls were mostly bare whitewash with only the window shutters and ornate iron grills as original fittings. Some of the rooms still had their colourful tiles and carvings in place, but not many. Interestingly, that 77mm Krupp field gun that was gifted to the Glaoui family for their kasbah at Telouet as payment for helping the Sultan back in 1893 (which was a key turning point for the start of the family's rise to power) had been subsequently moved from Telouet and was now stationed at the Kasbah Taourirt. While the kasbah was an interesting diversion, our real goal in Ouarzazate was to try and find examples of traditional Berber pottery and perhaps even a traditional potter or two.

***

Back in 1955, after leaving Idirh, Humphrey had split from his other team members and set off from Telouet with anthropologists Ernest and Susan Gellner whom he had met by chance at the kasbah. His intention was to try and expand his study of traditional Berber pottery by visiting some of the famous pottery sites located in the south. On his return to the UK, he even had an article published in the journal *MAN* (*The Monthly Record of Anthropological Science*) detailing his research and discoveries. By his own admission, while in Morocco, his interest in pottery was from an angle of naivety:

> Humphrey: "I was no expert in pottery but I had spent some time in Oxford with a man called Fogie and he gave me some notes on studying pottery on expeditions and so I did have some technical knowledge."

One of Humphrey's study areas was a potter community located just outside Kasbah Taourirt in Ouarzazate. He made some detailed observations of (among other things) how the clay for the pots was chipped out of a hillside some 3km away; how the potters' wheels were set in a pit in the floor with the operator sat on a ledge cut into the wall of the pit; how the pots were painted or glazed but never both; and the use of galena (a lead mineral) to create the glaze.

Potters of Taourirt ©Humphrey Beckett OUESM 1955

With a copy of Humphrey's illustrated article in my hand, we scoured the shops and roadside markets near Kasbah Taourirt for any examples of old traditional pottery but came up short. As far as we could tell, the area of Ouarzazate that used to be the pottery enclave (where Humphrey had conducted his studies) had since been built over and the potters moved on, so it wasn't looking very hopeful.

But then, something weird happened. Purely by chance, we noticed a doorway with what looked like old bits of pottery displayed outside the 'shop' (essentially a small cubicle area with a door that opened out onto the main road where all the pottery wares were displayed) and so we decided to investigate. A few men came up to us and we showed them Humphrey's magazine article and they looked interested. Then, one fellow said he had one of the specific shaped pots shown in the photos that accompanied the article. We asked if we could see it, of which he was more than happy to oblige and so we followed him off to his shop. True to his word, he had a number of very old pottery items that he said dated from the 1950s, each perfectly matching the examples Humphrey had illustrated or photographed for his article. The man said that his potters' wheel was still in its original setting, sunk down into a hole in the ground many decades earlier. The wheel certainly looked original and his shop (again, another small cubicle) appeared to have been built up around the wheel. Clearly, not all the potters had been evicted.

Then chance shined on us even more brightly. The current shopkeeper popped out and brought in another man who introduced himself as Aittasstift Ali. He had a look at the article and the photos and proudly announced that one of the images was of his father (Aittasstift Abdoulaah) and another was of his uncle (Aittasstift Brahim). We had found the son of the potters that Humphrey had studied during his time in Ouarzazate! What were the chances of that? We were blown away.

In his article, Humphrey had described a very specific painted Berber design comprised of thin, narrow lines and dots painted inside the bowls. Moving on to Aittasstift Ali's own shop, we saw that this type of design was still prevalent in the wares he made, and I managed to buy a couple of pieces showing it off to great effect.

It was wonderfully reassuring that in a world in constant change, there were some things that had stayed exactly the same. Our chance discovery of a potter and his pots, made in the same way his father and uncle had made them decades earlier, employing the same designs, was a little moment when we could once again reach back through time and make an incredible connection.

Modern Berber pottery still bearing the traditional designs

17

Gorges and Campervans

As I mentioned earlier, even before the students reached the village of Idirh, one of their number, zoologist Colin Pennycuick, left his teammates and set off with the famous explorer Wilfred Thesiger on a 300-mile trek across the Atlas Mountains. They set out with a guide and a mule and headed east. Colin told me they took no food with them nor did they have to buy any, for wherever they went, they were 'hospitably entertained' by Berber tribesmen, often spending their nights in the kasbahs of the local Sheiks or the houses of rich merchants. While on their journey, they made their way down to the market town of Boumalne and then on to the Dades and Todra (or Todgha) Gorges, located east of Ouarzazate.

By his own admission, Colin said he was never a great diarist and recalled that he had made very little notes during his walk alongside Thesiger. While he loved taking photos, from looking at his album of images, he only briefly snapped the two gorges, so I didn't have much to go on by way of original imagery from the time of the 1955 expedition. However, Todra gorge was one of the stops during my own youthful travels with tour group Exodus back in 1990, so at least I had my own images and experiences to compare and contrast, if only separated by seventeen years or so.

James and I secured transportation in Ouarzazate via a local hire car outfit and set off east towards the gorges.

If you recall, my 1990 trip was a huge, circular route travelling by truck around Morocco. The truck had been converted so that the group members (made up of ages ranging from me at seventeen, to one or two forty-plus solo travellers) could all sit in the back on long benches running down each side. Under each bench was a locker for our luggage (we were all fitted out with identical red Exodus barrel bags that perfectly fitted into the lockers), and the material sides of the truck could be rolled up to let the hot desert air rush past in a vain attempt to keep us cool. Approaching the Todra Gorge, I wrote in my diary how the truck had to ford several rivers – heavy rains had caused the rivers to swell and breach the roads. Once again, being the nascent naturalist, my diary was full of accounts of the wildlife I spotted, from countless frogs and toads, to sizeable white geckos and assorted bats. As we had done most nights during the trip, we camped out, but on this occasion, we were sleeping in large standing tents (designated as 'Arab' or 'Berber') that stood in the grounds of a hotel located within the gorge itself. We had a day free to explore the environs and I decided to leave the group behind and head off for a hike by myself – it was day twelve of the holiday and from my inklings, most of the people on the trip were starting to get on my nerves (and I theirs, no doubt).

Todra gorge cuts 400m deep through the surrounding orange/pink limestone plateau, with sheer, smooth walls rising up from the river running through it. It's actually made up of a series of wadis (river canyons) cut by the Todra river. In places, the canyon can be as little as 10m wide, making it quite a dramatic site.

My youthful hike took me up a mule path, out of the gorge itself, to traverse along the very top. En route I was often accompanied by a grey and black ground squirrel or two. From the sounds of my diary entry, I was certainly in need of a 'personal day'. I wrote:

Many thoughts. Hard to understand. Can't work things out. Will probably ignore them… and now very happy.

All a bit deep and lightly troubled, it seems, but at least I claimed to be happy, which is not a bad state of mind for a seventeen-year-old to be in.

I remember that the gorge was stark and barren. As I walked along the top, in the distance I spotted a Berber tent. Closer to hand (or rather, to foot), I was joined by some sort of desert mouse with an elongated proboscis for a nose. Having luncheoned in the shade of a large boulder, I then started my journey back down to the base of the gorge, but this proved tricky due to the sheer drops. I was now getting slightly anxious as I had run out of drinking water. To aid my descent, I discovered there were dry stream beds that cut into the side of the sheer gorge walls, and sliding down the polished rock surfaces, I slowly made my way down to the valley floor below. Parched and dehydrated, I picked up the pace. Arriving back at camp, I dropped my empty water bottle on the ground (I had planned on disposing of it appropriately) and started guzzling from a bottle I located from our truck. It was then that I got told off by the tour leader. This startled me somewhat – it was as if I was on a school trip being told off by a teacher, not a client on a holiday. It turned out, the leader, Neil, was in a foul mood. Word on the street was that he and one of the other paying clients (let's call her Ruth) had in fact got a room in the hotel the night before and details of their night-time shenanigans was the talk of the camp. But I digress.

Seventeen years later, James and I had driven out from
Ouarzazate to find and explore both the Todra and Dades gorges
as Colin had done, though we were in a hire car and not on
foot, nor were we accompanied by Wilfred Thesiger, one of the
greatest explorers of all time. Along the road were countless stalls
selling rocks and fossils, but the moment we stopped to have a
quick look (or indeed, just slowed down), we were accosted by
children demanding *un bon bon, un stylo, un crayon, un centime.*
Clearly, we were now on the well-trodden tourist trail. It was
a very different experience to our time staying in the Berber
village where no demands were ever made on us by the children
and indeed, they usually offered to help us.

En route, we stopped at the town of El Kelau M Gouna.
Unknown to us, it was market day, so we thought we'd have a
poke around. There was the usual spread of fruit and vegetables,
plus a couple of butchers selling assorted cuts of fly-strewn meat,
but we also happened across a cobbler, which was a bit of luck
as the sole on one of James's boots was slowly peeling off and
needed fixing. I must say, the cobbler did an excellent job and
the boot lasted for the rest of the trip. It was then that we noticed
some of the long, traditional Berber coats for sale. These were
made of very rough wool, brown in colour and looked exactly
like the hooded coat worn by Alec Guinness as Obi-Wan Kenobi
in *Star Wars*. We purchased one each.

After a picnic lunch on a bench near the car, we once again
set off. Driving along, I was amazed at the number of cyclists
everywhere and swarms of neatly dressed school kids, all in
smart western garb. This area was clearly a hub of education and
learning.

The first stop on our two-stop 'Gorges of Morocco Tour' was
the Dades Gorge. Sadly, this didn't live up to our expectations.
When Colin and Wilfred had visited, they had explored a section
that looked very dramatic, a little bit like a mini Grand Canyon,

with layers of canyons and gorges stretching off into the far distance. Maybe we just arrived at the wrong time of day, with the sunlight too high in the sky, thus obliterating the shadows which give large geology, like a gorge, the shape and form it needs for you to really appreciate its beauty. I speak here from experience as when my wife and I first visited the actual Grand Canyon in America, we arrived around midday on the Arizona side and it just looked flat, literally like someone had painted a large billboard with a picture of the canyon. We were a bit disappointed. But having got up to see the sunrise the following morning, it was then that the awe and wonder kicked in – it was all down to the light. Standing now with James at a lookout on the side of the road, the Dades Gorge was nice enough, but frankly it all looked a bit drab and not that interesting (even for someone like me who loves geology) and so we decided to drive on.

On the road, the bicycles and school children were now replaced by fleets of French campervans, all heading in the direction of our second, and hopefully more exciting, stop: the Todra Gorge. I seemed to remember that during my 1990 trip, there was just a single, lonely, isolated hotel. Not anymore. Making our final approach, which led us directly *into* this orange limestone ravine, there were now countless hotels lining the road.

Pulling up alongside seventeen huge motor homes (I counted them), we made enquiries and managed to book a room at the Hotel Yasmine. I wasn't surprised they had availability even at short notice, as I doubt they actually had much custom if most travellers arrived in a self-contained house-on-wheels with their beds already made up.

With sundown fast approaching, James and I headed out to explore the gorge, the stream that runs through it providing a refreshing humidity in the otherwise dry late afternoon air.

As you'd expect, in seventeen years not much had changed in something that had been there millions of years, at least as far as the geology was concerned. Given my previous experience of scrambling up the steep canyon walls and then almost getting stuck at the top, we decided to remain walking along the picturesque gorge floor. Much of the gorge was already in shadow, but we continued walking to a point where it opened out, and the sunlight still bathed the steep rock faces. This helped bring out the dark red of the rocks to juxtapose with the lush green of the palm trees growing alongside the stream. Most of the time we walked alone, but at one point we were accosted by two Berber women, one of which then decided to throw stones at her colleague for a reason we could not fathom.

Walking back to the hotel in twilight just before complete darkness enshrouded the gorge, we freshened up and had a lovely dinner out on the hotel's veranda. It was then that we decided to put on our newly purchased Obi-Wan Berber coats and wander out into the gorge once again. Sat alone in the darkness, we watched the sea of stars which now glowed across the dark sky. For a moment, we could have been the last Jedis (or perhaps a couple of Jawas) wandering the Jundland Wastes of Tatooine, hoping we wouldn't bump into any Tusken Raiders. Back at the hotel, the bed blankets were so heavy, it was like sleeping while being sat on.

18

Potters near the Dunes

Meeting the potters of Taourirt kasbah in Ouarzazate had already
given us a direct connection to one of the groups Humphrey had
studied decades earlier, but as part of his interest in traditional
Berber pottery techniques, he had continued to accompany
Ernest and Susan Gellner further south, to the town of Zagora
and then on to Tamegroute, home to a second company of
potters.

Zagora was a relatively modern town, built in the twentieth
century in the foothills of the nearby Zagora Mountain.
Tamegroute, on the other hand, was much older, dating from the
1500s and had been a religious centre since the eleventh century.
I discovered that it was the Nasiriyya religious brotherhood
that originally brought the potters (from the city of Fes) to
Tamegroute in order to improve the status of the village. While
Humphrey didn't make a detailed study of this specific group of
potters, he noted how they worked slightly differently to those
in Ouarzazate. Here, the pots were baked in huge ovens, glazed
in yellow and green using antimony and copper. I was keen to

find out what had happened to these potters fifty years after Humphrey and the Gellners had passed through, but our own journey of (re)discovery wasn't entirely straight forward.

I'd seen on our map that there was a route from the Todra Gorge, via a mountain pass, direct to Zagora. A man at our hotel thought it would be perfectly doable in our hire car, but I was wary the track may have required a more robust 4WD vehicle. Against my better judgement, we headed off, and soon enough the road became quite rough, so we decided to play it safe and double back on ourselves, taking the longer but more sensible route back via Ouarzazate and then down the Draa river valley. Along the way, whenever we pulled over to see the view or stop to buy water, we were instantly surrounded by children demanding biscuits.

The road down to Zagora was not the most relaxing of drives, with nightmare hairpin bends taking us up and over the assorted mountain passes of the High Atlas. En route, we were flagged down by a man standing next to what appeared to be his broken-down car. He explained that he was trying to get a lift to the town of Agdz. He didn't look like an axe murderer (but then again, does anyone?) and so we obliged. Arriving at Agdz, he insisted we have tea with him. We respectfully declined as we explained we were on a tight schedule and needed lunch, but he was quite persistent and said he would come and fetch us after lunch.

Agdz means 'Resting Place' and it's located back on the old caravan route from Marrakech to Timbuktu. It was rather green when we arrived, mostly on account of its position on the bank of the Draa river.

***

When the university students left the Berber village of Idirh, the party split up, with Bryan, Colin and Peter driving south.

When the trio arrived at Agdz, they were invited to stay with the French Commandant in the guest rooms of his fort. Bryan recalled in his book:

We did not expect, in this isolated place, a high standard of comfort. We were in for a surprise. A French soldier showed us to our rooms. Each of them was luxuriously appointed, there were thick carpets, modern paintings on the walls, very comfortable double beds, electric lights and private bathrooms... the fort bore a strong resemblance to the Ritz.

The group spent a day or so out in the nearby palm groves collecting animals. They dug up earthworms and beetles, chased butterflies, caught lizards and even managed to bag an elephant shrew, whom they named Willis. Bryan's description of the town made it sound like some sort of desert nirvana:

Agdz was at its best in the evening. The colours were heightened, the light was soft, people came out of their houses and moved about in the shade of the palms... there was an atmosphere of relaxation and friendliness.

For us, Agdz was nothing like Bryan described in his book. We found it to be a rather pokey town with very little charm. Not wanting to upset our hitch-hiker in declining his offer of lunch, we managed to hide from his line of sight behind two large French motorhomes and then, after lunch, quickly sped off when he wasn't looking.

The route down to Zagora was slow-going and mostly quite dull, with little to see other than the odd palm tree and the occasional date seller stood by the side of the road. But then, on the final approach to the town, that all changed. Stretched out before us like some green, leafy ocean was the largest palmery I had ever seen, with palm trees growing from horizon to distant horizon. Sadly, I could find very little information about when this palmery was established and by whom, but needless to say, it must have been some time ago on account of its sheer size. As we stood there gazing at the floral magnitude of the view, a little boy came out of nowhere and started the usual *un bon bon, un stylo* etc. We said we didn't have any, whereupon he dropped his trousers, urinated right there in front of us and then walked off! Moments later, a man appeared from nowhere and we were offered the opportunity to buy dates. We politely declined, but he soon got his sales when a tour van pulled up and the occupants all made purchases.

Zagora was once again a rather charmless place, but our destination was the next village along, that of Tamegroute. It was here that we found the famous community of potters Humphrey and the Gellners had happened upon, and these potters were all still hard at it, unchanged, it seemed, over the intervening decades. Wandering around, one potter took it upon himself to show us the whole process, from potter's wheel to finished product. He explained that the clay was dug out from a nearby palmery and thrown on a wheel similar to what we had seen at Taourirt, with the potter sat in a hole in the ground.

The pots were then stored in a room for twenty-four hours, placed in the sun for an hour, then fired. The kilns were large, mud brick ovens and we were told their fires were kept burning night and day, reaching temperatures of around 1200 degrees Celsius. The view of the kilns was like something out of an apocalyptic Hollywood film, as belching from the ovens was copious amounts of acrid black smoke. Much of this may have come from the straw they shovelled in, but I also saw a lot of plastic being readied to be burnt – pretty nasty stuff if you were breathing in the toxic, smoky fumes all day long.

The end products were mostly plates and bowls of various sizes, plus water jugs, many bearing a distinctive bright green

Potter of Tamegroute

glaze, identical to the green glaze of the roof tiles we had seen atop the decaying kasbah of Telouet. Consulting Humphrey's published academic paper, I learnt how the Berber potters of the 1950s tended to use ground galena for their glaze, a naturally forming mineral of lead sulphide. When he got home to Oxford and put his sample pots through a detailed chemical analysis, it revealed the firing process gave the pots a pure lead glaze. Fifty years on, things had changed (possibly down to the detrimental effects of lead poisoning?) and one of the potters told us that instead of galena, he used manganese which, when fired, created the ubiquitous green colour. He went on to explain that nowadays they had expanded their colour palette – as well as green from manganese, there was yellow from saffron, blue from indigo and red from henna.

Again, it was quite a special moment to find these potters, talk to them, see the processes in action and discover how things had changed, or indeed mostly stayed the same, over the intervening decades. It once again allowed us to connect back through time to the Oxford University students, in this case Humphrey in the company of Mr and Mrs Gellner, and potentially stand in the same spot they'd stood five decades earlier, asking the same questions. But because of the noxious smoke, we didn't stand there for too long.

From the potters of Tamegroute, it was a short drive to the village of Tinfou to a strange-looking, rather lonely, free-standing sand dune located by the side of the road. It appeared completely out of place and artificial, just plonked there with no connection to any other sand dunes. I questioned whether it was natural or indeed manmade for the tourist trade, a trade which was immediately apparent on arrival – we were accosted by men with their camels offering overpriced camel rides out on this singular, lonely sand dune.

According to my map, we were now just 70km from the end of the road, and only 100km from the Moroccan-Algerian border. I felt rather sad that the great, ancient tradition of the Moroccan camel caravan, leading out from Marrakech, crossing the edge of the Sahara (bearing dates and spices) on great journeys to the likes of Timbuktu (a mere fifty-two days away, according to a battered road sign), had been reduced to taking tourists around a car park-sized sand pit. Away from the crowds, we scaled the dunes and enjoyed the sunset.

19

Hollywood of the Sahara

Retuning back to the town of Ouarzazate, we stumbled across
a little piece of Hollywood located just on its western outskirts.
It was an enterprise that wasn't around in the 1950s when
Bryan and his team were in Morocco, but we couldn't pass it by
without having a look. The billboard grandly proclaimed that we
had arrived at the Atlas Film Studios, named (obviously) after
the nearby mountains. Another sign in the car park made the
bold claim that it was the world's largest film studio (measured
by acreage), with various famous film sets dotted about the
adjoining desert landscape.

The studio itself was set up in 1983, but the presence of some
really old film sets (now decaying under the hot Moroccan sun)
suggested filming in some form had been going on here well
before that. When we rolled up at the rather empty car park, the
site was looking tired and faded. The peeling billboard promised
'A great day out for all the kids'. I'm not sure if any family could
stretch it to the whole day as, in the end, we only managed forty-
five minutes.

Joining a guided tour, we were taken to see several film sets, such as the *Ten Commandments* TV mini-series, shot the previous year, which had starred Omar Sharif, plus a huge Egyptian temple used for filming the 1999 TV series *Cleopatra*, starring Timothy Dalton as Julius Caesar and Billy Zane as Mark Anthony. In the distance was the set of Jerusalem from the 2005 film *Kingdom of Heaven* with Orlando Bloom, plus the slave market from Ridley Scott's 2000 film *Gladiator*, starring Russell Crowe. There was also lots of paraphernalia from assorted *Asterix and Obelix* films (starring Gérard Depardieu as the menhir-carrying Obelix) which had also been filmed here.

All the old film sets weren't just there for visiting tourists to walk around – they are still used and reused by production companies from around the world who need a desert backdrop and are happy to hire and rejuvenate some old, weathered flats. More recent television series to have graced the existing film sets include *Game of Thrones* and *Vikings*. To be honest, without the film lights and set dressing, the eye and lens of a skilled Director of Photography and the VFX teams to digitally enhance the sets, it all looked a bit flat and pokey.

Slightly disheartened, our exploration of this desert Hollywood-land then stepped up a gear. Travelling further north, we came across another well-used film location, yet this was not a set made of plywood flats propped up in the desert, but a glorious, fully three-dimensional backdrop in the shape of the fortified town of Aït Benhaddou.

Aït Benhaddou is a *ksar* or fortified town, which dates from the eleventh century, built using bricks made of compressed earth and mud (also known as 'rammed earth') and was the home to one of el Glaoui's *Khalifas*. It was a significant stop for traders carrying gold, salt and slaves, travelling along the main caravan route to and from Marrakech and is now a UNESCO World Heritage Site.

When Bryan visited in 1955, he was told that he was the first Englishman to set foot in this remote town – how things had changed. When we rocked up, filming was taking place for a French film, *Alibaba*. Some years previous, Ridley Scott also came here and built a small amphitheatre arena type thing just in front of the town, in which he filmed Russell Crowe taking his first teetering steps to becoming a gladiator under the watchful eye of slave master, Oliver Reed. While we were there, teatime was called for the film crew and extras. They all trouped in to their catering tent, only to emerge seconds later with their food bags.

The *ksar* is made up of a set of interconnected and fortified houses built on a hill, with an ancient, destroyed granary (or *agadir*) perched right at the very top. Walking upwards through the narrow streets, it was immediately obvious this beautiful and picturesque desert town had become a centre for contemporary Moroccan arts and crafts. We saw many of the resident artists sat outside their shops (as they often do in places like this) working away. Many used a technique whereby they would paint on canvas using saffron and tea and then heat their artwork from below with a gas burner to effectively 'develop' the image. We also saw some artists burning designs in to wood using magnifying glasses – they certainly had the sun for it.

Climbing up the nearby hill to get a better view of the town, I found great big chunks of quartzite embedded in the clay earth substrate. These crystals (which can be found in quite large lumps) are made when quartz-rich sandstone is heated and put under pressure through tectonic compression. This act of geological metamorphism causes the sand grains and the silica cement that binds them together to recrystalise, creating the quartzite. As you should be aware by now, I do enjoy a nice bit of geology, and Morocco is a country that kept on giving.

After our brief detour to explore this Hollywood-land of the

Sahara, it was back on the road northwards, to visit the kasbah of Tamdaght. This was another glorious castle back in the day, where Bryan, Colin and Peter had been invited to stay as guests of another of el Glaoui's *Khalifas*. When el Glaoui was ousted in 1955, unlike most of his other kasbahs which were ransacked by the locals and then left empty to rot, we learnt that this one was initially taken over by a number of Berber families. Despite that, the rooms now had very little original detail left and the buildings had suffered terribly with age. While the kasbah still stood as a solid piece of Moroccan architecture, its walls were crumbling and bare of any detail, and the white plaster that had once covered the ramparts was long gone. A few good-looking blue doors were still in place, plus a balcony or two, but other than that, just blank, mud brick walls. Walking around, the site was all very sad, with great arched doorways now blocked up with ugly concrete breeze blocks. Leaving Tamdaght, it was a short drive back to Marrakech to catch the plane home.

20

Return (Again) to the Berber Village

Two years after I first followed in Bryan Clarke's footsteps, tracking down the Berber village his team of students had studied in the High Atlas of Morocco, I wanted to go back again. This time, I decided to take a video camera with me (along with our stills cameras), the plan being to see if I could make a short video documentary about life in the Berber village of Idirh.

As was the case when James and I made our first trip, I was still in the employ of the BBC television science department, at that time working on a big science series exploring the planets and moons of our Solar System, presented by the ex-keyboard player of Manchester pop group D:Ream and now CERN physicist, Prof Brian Cox. My episode was all about how the planets and moons live and die (geologically speaking) and Prof Cox and I had flown around the world filming various sites on Earth that were analogues (in some fashion) to places out in our Solar System. This included the giant (dormant) volcano of Mauna Kea (with all the huge telescopes on top) on the Big Island of Hawaii, an analogue of the giant extinct volcano of

Olympus Mons on Mars. We'd also been to mainland USA to explore the Grand Canyon (to compare with the vast Valles Marineris on Mars) and to the city of Middlesboro in Kentucky, the site of a giant meteorite crater whose centre of impact, so the local scientist informed us, was around the eighth hole of the town's golf course. En route, we discovered the town was home to none other than Lee Majors, *The Six Million Dollar Man*. I'd also been back to that molten lava lake in Ethiopia, this time to represent an analogue of Jupiter's violently volcanically active moon Io and, stepping in for a colleague working on an episode about our sun, I had filmed a total solar eclipse across the Ganges River in India. My film edit was coming to a close and so in November 2009, I managed to once again rope in my nephew James (who was now an Estate Agent), and we booked flights to Morocco.

Quite by chance (or indeed neglect in my organisational awareness), while I was sat on the plane thumbing through my guidebook, I discovered that we would be in Morocco during the time of Eid al-Adha, the Muslim Festival of Sacrifice, one of the most important festivals in the Muslim calendar. The festival celebrates the prophet Ibrahim's (Abraham's) willingness to sacrifice his son Ismael (Isaac) when God ordered him to. I was a bit concerned that we wouldn't be welcomed into the village during this time of celebration, but I'd written ahead to our original host Sharouk, asking if we could stay with him again, so he knew we were coming. Being in the village at this special time would certainly allow us to see and experience another important facet of Berber life.

Landing in Marrakech, we realised it was a completely new airport, and unlike our previous visit where our map had caused issues, this time we just walked straight through. Transportation into the centre of town was also incredibly easy, with a new bus service offering a return for just thirty dirhams each, dropping us off right at the famous Djemaa el-Fna. We'd chosen to stay at the same economically priced hotel (Sherazade) and weirdly, we were put in room eleven (again). So far so good.

This time round, I decided that we wouldn't employ a guide but just get ourselves to Taddert, see about organising a mule for our bags and walk into the valley by ourselves. I'm blessed (and cursed) with quite a good photographic memory and this, along with the actual photos I had taken on the previous trip (many of which I'd printed out to use as an aide memoir), I felt we should be able to successfully navigate back to the village of Idirh. My only worry in all this was that I hadn't had a reply from Sharouk to my letters telling him of our proposed trip. But you know, *insha'Allah*.

I planned for us to take a bus to Taddert, but immediately, we hit a problem. Having found the Marrakech bus station, we discovered that because of the festival of Eid al-Adha, everyone was going home (fairly obvious if I had thought about it), and the man at the bus station informed us that all the buses were full. Disaster! But then, a shady-looking ticket tout came up to us and said he could get us tickets for a bus. We politely rejected his offer but thought, if he had tickets then surely, the buses couldn't all be full? Following a bit of frantic toing and froing, enquiring at the various windows of the bus station, we once again came to the conclusion that yes, all buses out of Marrakech were indeed all full. So how could the ticket tout man's bus exist? Back he came to try to convince us to buy his magical bus tickets and said it would be 120 dirhams to Ouarzazate and then 120 dirhams to Taddert. I now felt a bit desperate (how else could we get to the village?). We coughed up the money, but on further interrogation, the man couldn't stick with a time for the bus's departure – 7:30, 7:00, 7:15? We said we'd see him tomorrow, but having paid for the tickets, I was now quite concerned. Did this magical bus even exist? Would our tickets be valid? Had we just fallen foul to the easiest scam possible? Would we ever get to Taddert, let alone the Berber village?

Over dinner in a little restaurant just off the vibrantly active Djemaa el-Fna, James and I talked over the issue of the mystery bus ride we'd just booked, of the Muslim festival of Eid and my growing anxieties of finding ourselves potentially stranded in the middle of nowhere with no transportation forwards or back. As was often my way, I descended into a little vortex of indecision, undermining myself, questioning my decisions, trying to go through every possible permutation of all possible outcomes and, as you'd imagine, getting myself tied up in knots, ultimately leading to confusion and uncertainty. Despite the fact we had already paid for the bus trip, it suddenly dawned on me that by far the safer option would be to try and hire a car – why hadn't I thought of that earlier?

Given the wide unknowns about the validity of our bus tickets (or even when our magical bus would be leaving Marrakech and if we would be allowed on it), we resolved that a hire car *was* the only solution and, given that I had driven in Morocco the last time we were here and suffered no mishaps, it was just the initial part of exiting the city that might be a bit scary.

We were in luck, and despite the mass movement of peoples returning to their ancestral homes for Eid, the following morning, we managed to secure a car. Navigating out of Marrakech turned out to be fairly easy, driving round the outskirts of the city and then off on the N9 road that would take us down to Taddert. We were on our way.

21

A Warm Welcome

It was an uneventful drive up to the mountain town of Taddert, where we once again met Hussein, the owner of the famous Auberge des Noyers. I gave him some of the photos of his auberge that we'd taken on the previous trip and, now armed with a video camera, he allowed us to film his roadside inn, its shady terrace and environs. We explained to him why we were back and that we planned to walk into the valley to visit the village of Idirh once again and mentioned that we'd like to hire a mule to carry our bags into the valley. I was also now a little wary of relying entirely on my so-called excellent photographic memory to navigate us to the village, so perhaps he knew someone who could guide us? Before long, a chap turned up who said he could supply both mule and guide and with a handshake, the deal was done.

We arranged with Hussein to leave our hire car outside his inn and ordered a vegetable tagine for lunch, consumed on his famous terrace boasting those marvellous views down the valley. The mule chap with whom we had struck our couriering deal then came back saying we should walk on ahead and he'd drive our bags to Idirh. We enquired as to when our bags would arrive. 'At some point', came the answer! We declined that offer for fear we'd never see our bags again, but he then revealed there were no mules available that day. However, he mentioned that he could provide a guide in the form of a small boy and our bags would come by mule later in the afternoon. Sigh.

As time was pressing on, we decided that between the two of us, we could carry our three large bags (two rucksacks and a barrel bag) and try to walk in without mule or guide. But then, a few minutes later, the child's father came up to us and said that the boy would guide us and he would bring our third bag (which now just carried our traditional Berber Obi-Wan cloaks, jumpers and some presents for our host), and we could expect him around 4pm that afternoon. He assured us he would deliver our bag to the village of Idirh, to the house of Sharouk Mohammed, *insha'Allah*! He sounded so confident that we agreed.

Leaving our hire car in the care of the auberge owner, we set off carrying our rucksacks (and water bottles), leaving our third bag with the new mule man to bring along later (on a mule, possibly), being led by a small boy, who couldn't speak English or French, into the vast barren, desolate mountain valley. What could possibly go wrong?

The rough dirt track leading off into the mountains was a half hour walk back down the main tarmac road from Taddert. But would you believe it, as we turned off the road onto the path, we came across seven mules sitting around, clearly unoccupied for the day. Sigh (again). But given we were now one bag down (the courier of which had walked off once we had struck the deal), plus there was no one around attending the said sleepy mules, we decided to press on.

Around us, the views started to look quite familiar, and I

am pleased to say we were able to use the photos I had taken from the previous walk in to double check we were going in the right direction. It's not that we didn't trust our young guide, it's just that we had no real idea if he knew we wanted to go specifically to the village of Idirh and not one of the other villages in the valley, or indeed that he even knew which village *was* Idirh. After all, our guide Talib from our previous excursion hadn't heard of the village and didn't really know where it was, asking the various villagers we bumped into along the way for directions. A few cars loaded with passengers passed us going both ways along the dirt track, so clearly, vehicular access to the valley was fairly frequent now, at least when it was dry and the roads weren't muddy quagmires. It crossed my mind that maybe we should have taken our chances and just driven in. But where's the adventure in that? And if we had driven in, we would have lost all that lovely connection we had with the students in 1955, who had walked in with their mule train following what was then *only* a narrow mule path.

James on the dirt road leading up and into the valley

A quarter of the way in, we arrived at the 'pass' (a ridge, if you like, where the dirt road then dropped down into the valley proper). At the pass now stood a massive mobile phone mast, which wasn't there when we came through two years previously. In many ways, walking away from the modern hustle and bustle of a town like Taddert (OK, some hustle but not so much bustle) into the High Atlas Mountains still felt like we were walking back in time, yet the march of technology was becoming ever more evident.

Walking on, the small boy indicated that we needed to turn off the main track and led us up and along a narrow path. This was the track we had ignored two years ago as our then guide Talib said it was 'broken'. But it might have been 'fixed' since then? Ten minutes later, a man came up from behind us and talked to the child. It transpired we had taken the wrong path, one that would lead us direct to the village of Titoula way up at the top of the valley and not to our wished-for destination of Idirh – I was correct in my assumption that a degree of some miscommunication would be encountered. Following the man's hand gestures, and after a little detour involving a very steep descent, we followed an equally narrow mule track that dropped down to arrive at a site directly opposite a village that appeared to look a lot like Idirh (I was still relying on our photos as aides for recognition). This then required a very strenuous hike back up the steep valley on the other side to get to the village proper. Fortunately, it soon became apparent we were in exactly the right place – we had arrived back in Idirh, our Berber village.

Walking in, I indicated to our young guide that I could now take over our navigation and managed to steer us successfully to our host's house. On arrival, we called up and were greeted by Mustafa and Khalid (the two youngest sons), plus Sharouk's oldest son who introduced himself as Hussein. There was a bit of confusion, but it was all of no consequence as we were received with a very warm welcome by Sharouk and were invited in for tea, bread and soup. Very little, if anything, had changed in the two and half years we'd been away and we were welcomed in like old friends – I was, of course, on the assumption that Sharouk had received my letter and was aware of, and indeed awaiting, our arrival (you can guess where this is going).

As expected, our third bag failed to turn up at the allotted time, but it was not a major hassle as we had envisaged such a possible delay. Back in Taddert, we had extracted what we thought would be all our 'essential' items prior to handing over the bag for mule delivery. I believed it just contained my towel, plus some pens and other presents we had brought to give to our host's children, but then I remembered it also contained all our cold weather gear, including our extra jumpers and our Obi-Wan Berber cloaks. Given that it was November in the High Atlas, the lack of warm clothing was a bit of an oversight (not so if we had taken delivery of our full complement of bags). A solution was provided by our host in the form of thick Berber blankets which, as always, were lovely and warm.

Given that the Berbers of Idirh love photos, we had an immediate session of showing updated pictures of my family and my sons, and while the gifts we had brought were in the missing bag (something that I could explain in French to the oldest son Hussein), I did have one little present to hand: a toy London Black cab, which I gave to the youngest son Khalid. He was very excited by that. We also met middle son Saeed again, who was now much grown.

Word of our missing bag had spread, but sadly, our only connection to the bag was the father of the boy who guided us in, whose name I could only recall was Mohammed. Not entirely helpful. I left the bag's recovery in the very capable hands of our host.

Following tea, we sat in Sharouk's living room for some considerable time under the thick, warm blankets and watched a film in English, *The Message about Prophet Muhammad*, during which, James fell asleep. A dinner of chicken and rice was brought out, after which we tucked down for bed, with an evening viewing of WWF wrestling slam down. It felt rather incongruous watching beefed-up, oiled American wrestlers playing out their wrestling pantomime as we sat with our Berber friends high up in the Atlas Mountains. Still, entertainment is entertainment and the kids and Sharouk seemed to enjoy it. I found it rather difficult to sleep that first night – I felt I could have benefitted from a thicker mattress and a more forgiving pillow.

Breakfast came in the form of the green tea slash hyper-sugar drink, plus bread and cheese. Whereas on the last trip we only had stills cameras, this time I was able to capture everything on video, trying to build up a narrative of moving imagery, showing a typical day in the life of the Berber village.

After breakfast, I had to attend to James's feet, as the walk in had caused some serious blisters to emerge. With his blisters now dressed, we set off with Mustafa (our host's second youngest son who was very interested in our video camera) and aimed for a narrow mule path we had seen during the walk from Taddert. It gave incredible views across the valley where we could film the village set in its mountainous backdrop. Without our warm clothes, and despite putting on pretty much everything else we had with us, it was still fairly chilly, but Sharouk was kind enough to lend us a thick Berber coat each.

Pretty soon, just as had happened during our wanderings before, we had gathered a band of young boys, each getting cockier by the minute. The morning light was glorious, and Mustafa insisted on carrying my camera tripod. It wasn't long before he became very adept at setting it up and then setting up the camera clamped on top.

Enjoying the warmth of a thick Berber coat (aka the Obi-Wans)

Along the way, we stumbled upon a walnut tree. The boys immediately scooted up the trunk and started throwing down the nuts which, without a bespoke nutcracker, we turned to the age-old method of cracking them open (developed long ago by our simian ancestors) by banging them with a rock. Very tasty they were too.

After filming for an hour or so, we returned back to the house. Completely by chance (or by the will of a higher authority), our host Sharouk had come across a teenage American-speaking Berber Moroccan by the name of Othman. He was a tenth grader who said he was out with a chap who was preparing to install pipes to carry water into the village and take sewage out. Strangely enough, I completely forgot to ask *why* this teen schoolboy was out with a chap preparing to install water and sewage pipes and just assumed (as was often the case) that they were related in some way. But then it hit me – did he just say water and sewage? Were the villagers at last getting access to running water on tap? And with the construction of a sewage system, would more homes soon have some sort of household lavatory installed? Or perhaps to begin with, would there be a village standpipe or two, set up for individual households to collect their drinking water, as opposed to using the stream, and maybe a communal toilet block? Sadly, (and I must apologise for my lack of journalistic rigor) I simply forgot to interrogate this further. Still, it leaves open another potential chapter to this story and perhaps a reason to return in the future to see what effect said running water and sewage disposal might have on the further development and modernisation of the Berber village.

Othman had very good English and was more than happy for us to use him as a translator, which helped no end as communication was always our biggest hurdle – we had no Arabic or Berber and we could only just about get by in French. Through our young translator, we now discovered that our host Sharouk had in fact *not* received any of my letters and so was quite surprised when we turned up out of the blue. Fortunately, that hadn't fazed him in any way. Given that we had also arrived at the time of the Eid celebrations, I politely asked if it was OK if we stayed with him for Eid, to celebrate with his family and to document the celebrations. He said it would be fine. I also managed to ask (via Othman) about our missing bag. It turned out that Sharouk knew the boy that had walked in with us and knew his father and so he had made arrangements for the bag's safe arrival (*insha'Allah*, of course).

After a second breakfast of bread and oil, everyone dressed in their finest djellaba to go to the village mosque for Friday prayers. We wandered down with the family, then went for a walk, filming more of the village. A chicken tagine lunch followed (as I said before, life in the Berber village generally revolved around food and drink, which was not a bad thing), then an afternoon walk with Mustafa and Khalid to get more shots of the town, plus a time-lapse sequence framed up across the valley to capture the movement of the mountain shadows cast by the setting sun. At this stage of my proposed video documentary about life in the Berber village, I was just excited to get out and capture a sequence of shots, as I had no real idea how I might use them, or the narrative the film might follow. But it was fun being out with our host's youngest sons, who seemed to be very interested in the whole filming process.

22

Celebrating Eid

It was the day of Eid al-Adha. As everyone had dressed up in their finery, I offered to take a family portrait, which, this time, included Sharouk's wife and daughters. We were then asked to accompany the men and boys as they walked up the valley to a special wide-open area just outside the village. It was here that the town's menfolk (mostly dressed in white) took part in communal prayer. The men stood together on large mats that had been laid out on the dusty ground, with all the boys (mostly still dressed in their standard western clothing) clustered together in one corner. Soon the Imam started prayers. We stayed some distance away as I was aware that as westerners and non-Muslims, perhaps this should be something private to the village. But our host insisted that we were welcome to watch and film, so we did, but at a respectful distance.

Back in 1955, Bryan and his team were also witness to the Eid al-Adha celebrations in Idirh, which that year happened at the end of July. It was Colin who noted that, at that time, both the men *and* the boys of the village dressed in their finest white

The menfolk of Idirh congregating on a hilltop just outside the village

djellabas before attending prayers. Just like us, the students felt a little self-conscious of their presence in the village at this very important time in the Muslim calendar, more so given the political situation in Morocco. Bryan wrote:

Eid… is also the occasion for excesses of religious fervour (often taking the form of the elimination of infidels) and the French authorities had advised us to be circumspect during the festivities.

For us, the prayers went by without incident, except for some boisterousness exhibited by the young boys who perhaps were a bit bored by it all. At the end of the prayers, there were lots of 'peace be with you' type greetings, and then we followed the crowd as they walked back down to the town square. A gentle chanting arose, and all the boys lined up to give the Imam a coin or two. I also saw that money was being handed to the older fellows in

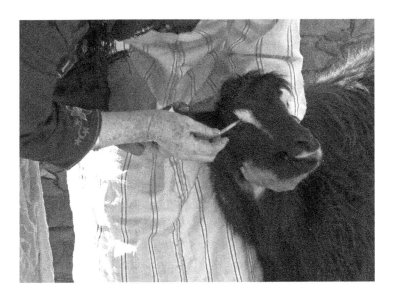

The sacrificial goat has some eyeliner applied

the crowd. I was told by our host (through Othman, our happy-to-help interpreter) that charity and the giving of gifts was a key part of Eid al-Adha. A large bowl of circular biscuits were also set down on the floor and people helped themselves. I noted they were similar in shape to the top half of a Jammy Dodger.

Back at the house, it was straight up onto their roof terrace where our host prepared for the sacrifice, which in Idirh would be a goat as opposed to a sheep, which I was told was the preferred animal in the wider Muslim world. Looking across the town's rooftops, I could see that every family was now preparing their own goat for the sacrifice. We were soon joined by our host's wife, who force-fed the goat with a handful of grain and then appeared to put some sort of mascara on its eyes.

Meanwhile, the youngest son Khalid was given the honour of holding the special sacrifice knife. I noticed that Sharouk had now changed out of his white finery and had put on a coverall – clearly, things were going to get messy.

Back with the goat, Mrs Sharouk continued with some ceremonial water action (which I assumed was a cleansing process?) and then the village butcher arrived, who had been going from house to house. The goat was held, its throat cut and the blood allowed to drain out. Its head was then cut off.

Neither James nor I had ever seen a butcher at work, let alone one involved in a religious sacrifice, so it was a bit of an eye-opener. We watched (and filmed) in fascination as, following the exsanguination, a small bamboo tube was inserted into a cut in the animal's leg. This was then blown into, which (we were informed) helped separate the skin from the muscle. The butcher then skinned off the rear end and the goat was hooked up by the tendons in its feet and the skinning continued. I was amazed at how fast it all happened. The removed skin was eventually separated from the underlying fat layer, and this was then proudly placed on the shoulders of Mustafa (the second youngest son) to dry out, I assumed as part of the ongoing ceremony.

Meanwhile, back with the goat carcass, the guts and organs were extracted (but not discarded). We were then ushered down from the roof terrace to the main living room where a small, portable barbeque had been set up. The goat's liver (still warm from being inside the goat) was wrapped in a layer of its own fat and cooked there and then. As you can imagine with an inside BBQ, smoke soon filled the room. While not a big fan of liver, I must admit it tasted amazing.

We were then told to wrap up and were directed out of the house. It would appear the afternoon's entertainment was about to start, as we were led to the outskirts of the village where a football match was getting ready to kick off. A large, flat area had been cleared of rocks and debris, and a fair-sized football pitch created. I assumed this was a special Eid football match, possibly between villages? We watched (and cheered both sides), sat with the youngest boys, as the match itself was reserved only for the older teens.

As dusk took hold, back in the town the sound of drums and singing wafted through the air. We found out that this was the beginning of something called an *Ahwash*, a form of traditional collective performance that is known throughout the Berber tribes of southern Morocco, and possibly even had its origins in nearby Telouet. From what I understood, the songs often had some pre-Islamic components in them, drawn from traditional Berber religion. An Ahwash is a very spiritual part of any celebration, and we were incredibly privileged to see it.

Again, we stayed a respectful distance and didn't want to appear like we were gawping at the festivities. Instead, we enjoyed listening to the chorus as we took tea on the roof of Sharouk's brother's house, located just off the town square where the Ahwash was now in full flow. The square was packed, made up of the teenagers and young men and women of the village. I recorded what turned out to be a twenty-three-minute song, which started with the girls and was then taken over by the boys and then had a whole Q and A session (back and forth) between the boys and the girls.

It was while we were sat drinking tea that we were told (by Sharouk's older sons, who had a good grasp of French) that a small number of youths from the village had taken offence at our presence. I thought this was quite understandable, what with us turning up out of the blue (due to my letters never getting to our host) and being in town at one of the most holy times in the Muslim calendar. However, we were reassured by the elders that the specific teen boys were 'racist' and that we were very welcome in the village at this special time.

***

Fifty years earlier, Bryan also witnessed an Ahwash as part of the Eid al-Adha festivities, and again, similar to us, he felt that perhaps he shouldn't have been there:

> Bryan: "We went to the Ahwash and I got the heebie-jeebies because I thought this was a ceremony where you cleansed and removed evil by dancing and I thought they were going to cleanse the village of the evil brought in by us. At least that's what I thought was being planned. Anyway, it didn't happen needless to say."

From what Bryan described in his book, and comparing that with what we were now witnessing in the village square, the ceremonial singing that made up a significant component of the Ahwash hadn't changed in the intervening decades:

> *The singers were divided into groups and each would begin or end a fragment of the song, seemingly at random. But I soon realised that although the fragments might in themselves be meaningless, they were contributing to the drama of the whole. Human voices were serving as instruments in an orchestra to create an effect far more impressive than any simple melody. There was a heightened emotion in the swelling voices which conveyed their rejoicing in the occasion.*

Sat as we were on a roof just off the main square, Idirh's young people carried on singing well into the night, but we couldn't keep our eyes open, so we decided to turn in. Returning to our host's home, we discovered that our wandering third bag had finally arrived from Taddert, so that evening we could finally wear our *own* djellabas (aka the Obi-Wan cloaks). Despite the slight air of discontent about our presence in the town at this special time, we now felt right at home.

23

Final Farewell

Our days in the village were mostly spent filming, eating, drinking mint/green tea and repeating the cycle. As before, the morning and late afternoon light was beautiful, the 'Golden Hour' as it is known in the trade, but given it was November and the sun arced low over the sky, we were blessed with many such golden hours. Some of the time, we were joined by a small band of boys who insisted on carrying our kit for us. Other times, we wandered around alone, sitting out in the valley, enjoying the stillness and breathing in the clear mountain air.

With our time in the village once again coming to an end, we made preparations to depart. Now that we had regained our missing bag, I could give out the presents I'd brought from England. This mostly centred on pens and pencils, toys for the young sons and a handsome, thick hoodie for our host, which were all well-received.

It was a joy to have returned to the Berber village, to be welcomed back into Sharouk's home like an old friend (despite the fact he had no idea we were coming), to spend time with

The Berber Village

his young sons and show them how to work our cameras, and to celebrate that most special time of Eid with the family. We had built on our knowledge and understanding of the way of life in Idirh and cemented our friendship with our most generous host.

Having said our goodbyes, we set off on the mule path back to Taddert. The boy that had guided us into the village was apparently going to come and guide us out, but we had no idea when he was meant to turn up (if at all) and so we left by ourselves (sharing the burden of carrying our third bag), fairly confident we could retrace our steps back to the main road. We were joined by Mustafa, who walked with us for some of the way.

It was a fairly strenuous walk with steep climbs to get back out of the valley, often with a precarious ledge just to the side of the narrow mule/goat path. At the pass, we had a frugal lunch of bread and butter, honey and nuts. Our plan now was to drive off to revisit Telouet in the hope that we would be allowed to

A final farewell to Sharouk, our generous host in Idirh

film inside the kasbah, so during our lunch break, I took full advantage of the existence (and proximity) of the mobile phone mast that towered above us. Going online, I found a little inn at Telouet called the Lion d'Or Auberge. Calling them from atop the ridge in the High Atlas, I booked a room for me and James – isn't technology marvellous! Bryan and his team had been completely isolated when they spent their summer in Idirh, but for us, the outside world was now accessible at the touch of a button.

With a final look back along the valley, we stepped over the ridge and once again left our Berber village behind.

Following the track back to the main road, we saw no one except for a single orange minibus packed full of people heading into the valley. In Taddert, the only shop that was open was staffed by the guy that had organised our child guide (had he been waiting for us?). We paid him a small fee for looking after the hire car (which was all present and correct) and fifty dirhams for the delivery (albeit very late) of our extra bag. Leaving Taddert, we drove off to Telouet via a narrow road which snaked through an orange, red and yellow lunar looking landscape, ironically with the actual moon hanging large and low overhead.

The Lion d'Or Auberge sat right next to the kasbah of Telouet. Checking in, we had arranged for dinner, bed and breakfast all for just 160 dirhams each. Safely installed in our room, it was here that my body finally ended its four days of (psychologically enforced?) constipation, which, I'm sorry to be blunt, was totally fabulous. We then spent the afternoon and evening wandering around outside the kasbah, filming in the glorious golden light.

The following morning, the sunrise was a riot of colour as is often the case in desert climes. After breakfast, it was out to try and gain access to film inside the kasbah. Unlike our last visit, where we had to actively seek out the Guardian, this time the aged Berber key master had a little stall set up near the massive front gates and charged twenty dirhams entry. On this occasion (perhaps because he was expecting further visitors?), once he had unlocked the main doors, we were allowed to wander around unaccompanied. While it was nice to film the rooms rather than just take stills as we did before, without some sort of activity going on, it was a little bit like filming wallpaper. What we needed were some fabulous actors in lavish costumes acting out the final days of the decline and fall of the Glaoui family. Maybe next time?

With the arrival of rain, we felt we'd had enough of this second trip down memory lane. Heading back to the auberge, through what was a rather eerily quiet town, we paid up, packed up and left.

The drive back to Marrakech was mostly uneventful, slipping into and out of clouds that topped the higher ground. En route, we stopped to buy some chocolate and fossils at a high pass known as Tizi n'Tichka, which stands at an elevation of some

2260m and has the accolade of being the highest mountain pass in North Africa. Apparently, it was also the last known location of the last known wild Barbary Lion living in Morocco, which was shot near the pass in 1942.

In Marrakech, we off-hired the car and headed back to our original hotel (Sherazade), then stepped out for a wander. Othman, the American-speaking Berber boy that we had met (by chance?) in Idirh (who had acted as our most excellent translator) had mentioned that his father owned a small hotel in Marrakech (Hotel Ali) and that we should drop in for a session in their hotel's private hammam. Do you see where I'm going with this 'by chance' business? We were very well looked after on our trip, from our host welcoming us to stay even though he didn't know of our impending arrival, to having the wonderful and privileged opportunity to film the Berber Eid festivities and be with our Berber family at that special time, to having a young translator rock up out of nowhere, who not only helped us no end with our communication issues, but then invited us to partake in a hammam at his dad's hotel. *Insha'Allah* – there is certainly something in it.

Neither James nor I had ever been to a traditional Moroccan hammam, so we were keen (and anxious) to see what it was all about. We met Othman's father and arranged to go back that evening. Exploring the souk located just off the Djemaa el-Fna, we made a few small purchases, then it was back via the square (past a film crew) to the Hotel Ali and the exotic delights of the hammam.

The hammam was quite an experience. Stripping down to our boxers, we were led into a hot room and instructed to wash. Then our attendee, a man in tight, red Speedos, gesticulated for us to lie flat on the heated floor. He then proceeded to rub us with black soap, rinsed us, then rubbed us with a rough glove – you could see the dirt and skin sloughing off. We were rinsed again and then our hair was washed and rinsed, then rinsed again. We both agreed that we had felt quite vulnerable lying there almost completely naked while being manhandled, but it was fabulous. We came away very clean indeed.

We were then invited upstairs for dinner as Othman's guests – he really was the gift that kept giving. Despite offering, he wouldn't accept a penny (or a dirham) and we had an amazing dinner. The evening was rounded off with a final saunter around the square, then back to our hotel.

It had been a short trip this time, a chance to briefly revisit Bryan's Berber village. We had returned with some of the photos we'd taken the first time round in the knowledge that the villagers loved a photo; we had witnessed and been part of the holy Eid celebrations; we had seen and heard the unique Berber Ahwash; I had been able to shoot many reels of video footage that I hoped I could fashion into some sort of short documentary about life in Idirh; and we had further built on our friendship with our host and his family. I would later write to Sharouk, sending yet more photos and presents to thank him again for his hospitality. I mentioned to him that I hoped to write a book about the 1950s expedition and our own journey of rediscovery to locate and return to the Berber village of Idirh. At the time, I wasn't aware just how long it would take to write the book, but I knew someday I would finish it, *insha'Allah*.

24

Back Home

As the summer of 1955 was drawing to a close, the time came for the university students to start making their long drive back to Oxford. The route took them via Marrakech, which they now saw with more enlightened eyes.

> Bryan: "After you've been in the mountains for a while, Marrakech is mind-blowing. I mean, it's the height of civilisation and all kinds of possible comforts and nice food and yet, when we first went there, we thought it was the back of beyond. But when you've been in the back of beyond, you can see why the inhabitants get really excited when they're going to Marrakech."

The team planned to get home the same way they had travelled to Morocco, driving all the way back in their rather untrustworthy truck, *Tartarin*. It took longer than expected. Back in Oxford, the group were already several weeks late, and a local newspaper ran the headline *Oxford Explorers Missing*. The author of the piece even hinted that the team had been massacred by Moroccan Nationalists. The reason for their delay (as was the case with all their delays) was down to their truck.

Humphrey would go on to write an article detailing *Tartarin's* various trials and tribulations in a magazine called *The Wide World: The True Adventure Magazine for Men*. This was quite a fascinating magazine (a copy of which Humphrey lent me), a real 'boys own' but for men. Its pages were filled with adverts for manly things like Solaross binoculars, Philishave shavers, tins of tobacco (Gallaher's rich dark honey dew) and Herbert Terry anglepoise lamps which, as the advert informed me, no self-respecting fly fisherman could do without to illuminate their workbench so they could accurately thread their fly-fishing flies. There were also adverts for Ye Olde Wood Barling pipes, Willerby caravans (for those men who are choosy about their caravans), men's Aertex underwear, assorted guns, a build-your-own canoe from Tyne Folding Boats Ltd and a 'manly' girdle which promised to take inches off your waist. There was even an advert for the Travel Book Club, which would later publish Bryan's account of their Moroccan expedition, a copy of which I would find in my parents' loft decades later.

Humphrey titled his report *Five Men and a Truck*, and the byline promised an *amusing and racy account of an adventurous journey* in which he detailed the expedition with a heavy bias on the problems beset them by their awful truck. He recounted that having left Marrakech and started on their long journey home, 40km outside of Tangier the engine fell out. It was only down to assorted trips to scrap yards and various amounts of welding and patchwork repairs that they finally got it going again and made it home.

Now safely back in Oxford, the political upheaval that Bryan and his team had witnessed in Morocco (albeit mostly indirectly) continued to unfold with frightening speed. Grandval, the incumbent French Resident General, stepped down, leaving the French authorities in Morocco effectively leaderless. It was also around this time that T'hami el Glaoui was diagnosed with cancer. In October 1955, Sultan Mohammed Aarafa finally abdicated amid moves to reinstate the exiled Mohammed Ben Youssef. Only now did el Glaoui finally meet with members of the Nationalist Istiqlal party in a vain attempt to switch allegiances. Blind and in constant pain, the aging warlord's health continued to decline. According to a report in *Time Magazine*, on 8th November 1955, el Glaoui went to Paris to pay homage to the Sultan, recently returned from exile in Madagascar, or in the words of the news article, he *grovelled to the Sultan begging forgiveness.* On his knees kissing the feet of the Sultan, the article reported that Glaoui declared it was his wish for the *restoration of Mohammed Ben Youssef and his return to the throne* and that he gave his full support to the Nationalist government.

With reconciliation in the air, the Sultan granted el Glaoui a pardon and promised royal protection for his heirs. Mohammed V (as he was then known) was welcomed back to Morocco and was proclaimed Sultan, a position he would hold until August 1957 when he was exalted to King Mohammed V of Morocco. Bryan reflected in his book:

> As an outsider, an observer, I could only marvel and regret the tragedy, a tragedy made the more poignant because it was inevitable. The Protectorate had within it the seeds of its own destruction and the resulting conflict could not conveniently be summed up in terms of black and white…
> In the darkness 'all the cats were grey'.

During their time in Morocco, either in the Berber village or travelling around, the team often had mixed emotions about the ongoing and inevitable process of change.

Bryan: "I was in Marrakech and I saw a magazine with photographs that was being sold with pictures of the massacre at Wassane and there were groups of people looking at these, and they were exalting at all these pictures of bloody French corpses and they were really chuffed about it. It really made me feel sick in the stomach. That was the point at which I felt least sympathetic to the Moroccans."

The students had set out to investigate the flora and fauna of the High Atlas Mountains and to study a Berber village. This they succeeded in doing, but they were also present in Morocco right at the moment of an often bloody and violent state of transition.

Bryan: "I don't think people appreciate how fragile civilisation is. I think that was something that impressed me in Morocco. When we first arrived, apart from a few scary moments, initially everybody seemed to be getting along alright, you know. And then, in a matter of two or three months, there were people driving around with guns pointing out of their cars because they were frightened that they would be attacked. And there were Frenchmen saying, 'we've got to kill them before they kill us' kind of thing."

Charles: "El Glaoui was certainly pro-French. And maybe the French allowed him a measure of independence and although the revolt was by Nationalists against the French, I don't believe that they won in the main part of Morocco, except that they more or less got rid of el Glaoui in the south."

Humphrey: "We were out for an adventure and I think

we were quite happy to ignore the political situation, but we couldn't. So I'd say we had to grow up a bit because life wasn't simply a matter for some young Englishmen having an adventure. We had to take all of this very seriously by the end. Apart from anything else, we realised our lives were dependent on it by then, because the situation developed so rapidly while we were there."

For T'hami el Glaoui, his cancer spread. He was flown to Marrakech and, on 7th December 1955, was operated on by French surgeons. On 23rd January 1956, following night prayers, he died aged seventy-eight. He was branded a traitor, France's chief collaborator and was (and possibly still is) despised by Moroccan nationalists. Even his name entered into folklore, the French word *Glaouise*, meaning 'betrayed', in that he betrayed his people.

On 2nd March 1956, Morocco finally gained its independence.

As my interview with Bryan was drawing to a close, he recalled how he and his expedition team were quite isolated from much of the political action:

Bryan: "We were innocents in the middle of all of it. At one point we were cut off completely from all communication for, I think, a month or two because they'd cut the telephone wires and the traffic had been stopped over the mountain paths. There were no letters coming through, there were no telephone calls and there was fighting going on in Marrakech. Then of course, people with bullet wounds started coming into our camp and we were treating them. They'd been in the fighting in the cities and it was then when the telephone wires got put back in and letters came, great piles of letters from home saying come home at once, we've heard all about these terrible goings on in Morocco and, you know, please come home."

At the time of Glaoui's death, he was thought to be one of the richest men in the world. The Glaoui family had reportedly amassed a fortune worth over $17m (equivalent to around $162m in today's money), with some of the wealth lodged as cash in banks in Paris, London and Geneva, plus countless houses and palaces across Morocco and assorted stock holdings in various mines. While Sultan Mohammed V initially pardoned el Glaoui, the same forgiveness was not granted by the now governing Istiqlal Party. It is alleged they used their secret police to seize Glaoui's sons, who were held until his estate could be examined. An article in *Time Magazine*, dated 20th May 1957, said the examiners were *researching the origin of wealth acquired by traitors*. Despite the Sultan's former act of forgiveness while T'hami was still alive, he too, soon changed his mind and, siding with the government, agreed that the sons had indeed been involved in anti-national activities and were to be stripped of their wealth.

Having returned to Oxford, Bryan and his team had a number of expedition-related jobs to do, from thank you letters, to writing reports for the University Exploration Club and their various sponsors, plus a number of magazine articles to send off. Being primarily a zoological expedition, the team had also collected a large number of specimens, including five hundred snails, four hundred earthworms, 4500 insects, forty reptiles, fifteen amphibians and five mammals. Most had been pickled and preserved and were handed over to the Oxford University Museum of Natural History, a glorious Victorian building located on Parks Road in central Oxford, to add to their collection. I wrote to the museum, and they confirmed they still had a small selection of pickled animals donated by Bryan from the 'O.U. Expedition to Southern Morocco'.

One specimen that was not pickled but kept alive and well, was a Barbary Ground Squirrel which had been caught near Idirh. In November 1955, Bryan gifted the squirrel to the Zoological Society of London.

As well as collecting zoological specimens from the area, the expedition had also set out with a variety of anthropological goals, mostly driven by Humphrey, including his study of traditional Berber pottery. A large collection of pots and potters' tools, plus rugs, other textiles and coins that he collected were donated to the Pitt Rivers Museum in Oxford, which adjoins the University Museum and houses the university's archaeological and anthropological collections.

In February 1956, Bryan gave the required illustrated talk about his expedition at the bi-weekly meeting of the Oxford University Exploration Club. I couldn't find any notes of how well his presentation had gone, but he was up against some stiff competition – the next illustrated talk to be held a couple of weeks later was to be given by a Mr David Attenborough, recounting his BBC filming expedition to Guiana.

Bryan also needed to wind up the expedition's finances. All in, the cost of the trip came in at £1088/0/8. This is equivalent to around £28,733 in today's money. I would say from my own time at Oxford and organising two OUEC approved expeditions, that by the 1990s, university expeditions cost significantly less. But then again, most expedition teams would jump on a plane and didn't drive thousands of miles in a dilapidated old truck to get to their study sites.

In all, the team travelled over seven thousand miles. Despite all the troubles with their truck, a glance at the expedition accounts revealed they managed to sell it on after they'd returned to Oxford for the sum of £150, three times what

```
            MEETINGS

       HILARY TERM 1956


   Thursday  2nd February
        Mr. BRIAN CLARKE will give an
       illustrated talk on the Oxford
       University Expedition to
       Southern Morocco 1955.
                        Emden Room S.E.H.

   Wednesday 15th February      OPEN MEETING
        Mr. DAVID ATTENBOROUGH  will give
       a talk illustrated by slides and a
       film on the recent B.B.C.-Zoological
       Society Expedition to British
       Guiana.
                   Joint Lecture Theatre
                   Dept. of Botany & Forestry.

   Tuesday 28th February
        Señor RICARDO LUTI will give an
       illustrated talk on two journeys in
       the Argentinian Andes.

                        Emden Room S.E.H.


       ALL  MEETINGS  AT  8.15 p.m.


            JOHN NEWBOULD

               Secretary.
```

The OUEC term card featuring Bryan's talk
(and a subsequent talk by Mr David Attenborough)

they paid for it. But then it had had a lot of work done to it by
then. Bryan had made a note that he thought the quality of the
original repair and overhaul work that had been undertaken
prior to their departure wasn't up to much. But then again, the
repair shop weren't happy about the original state of the truck.

I found an invoice from Hartwells of Oxford who were chasing Bryan for an outstanding payment. They noted:

We find it difficult to reconcile ourselves to the extent to which the trouble you experienced was attributable to the repairs carried out on the vehicle, bearing in mind the exceptional nature of the service to which the truck was being subjected, and its suitability for work. It is apparent to us that a second-hand vehicle of this type should have been completely stripped and overhauled throughout for a journey of this nature, if freedom from trouble was to be assured.

In his book's epilogue, Bryan became reflective:

It may be that I shall never be able to return to the valley, yet it has become part of me and I have an irrational half belief that events in Idirh and the fortunes of its inhabitants will affect me even over the miles that separate us.

He hoped that the villagers would remember him and his team and that the time the students spent in the village was sufficiently unusual to stay in their minds. Fifty years later, my own journey into the mountains to retrace the footsteps of the university expedition confirmed this had indeed been the case.

Continuing in his reflective note, Bryan asked *what had we achieved?* He listed the specimens they had collected; there was also a Berber blood abnormality Charles Pasternak had found within his own small research project at the hospital in Ouarzazate; Humphrey had uncovered some unique pottery glazes; plus there was their detailed account of life in the Berber village. He noted: *these seemed to be meagre results for the effort and expenditure which went into the enterprise*

But he believed the effort was justified:

We had learned a good deal from meeting people and situations that we would otherwise have missed. We had all grown a little wiser – not much but a little.

Epilogue

Bryan's book about the expedition (the book that started my interest in their story and the story of Morocco in 1955) was published in 1959. I discovered from several letters dated from 1958, that he had originally given his manuscript the title *The Naked Mountains*, which a man by the name of George Greenfield from John Farquharson Ltd (Business Managers for Authors) thought was 'a shade imprecise'. The same man noted in a letter to Bryan that, while he enjoyed reading the manuscript, he felt *it is not of course a wildly dramatic story as expeditions go, but I thought you had told it with clarity and a certain degree of grace of style which made for most pleasant reading.* A member of the publishing team from Longmans, Green and Co made the suggestion of an alternate title, that of *Berber Village*, which they felt *instructive, easy to remember and highly relevant.* Following the book's publication, the reviews were mostly positive:

The Guardian 25/9/59
It may well have helped to shape men who will contribute much more in the future... a worm's eye view of developing nationalistic feeling in a backward region under the rather nasty regime of el Glaoui just before his decline and fall.

Scotsman 16/5/59
There are undertones of serious and conscientious endeavour... his book makes capital reading.

Kentish Observer 13/8/59
This often naive (and so most likable) book is in the simplicity of the author's attitude towards life.

South China Morning Post 12/10/59
The author writing in an amusing and light-hearted manner gives a very interesting picture of life amongst these isolated Berbers.

Oxford Magazine 15/10/59
It stands out from the general ruck of books describing undergraduate expeditions by the vitality and gaiety of its writing.

For the Oxford University students, life back in Oxford soon returned to normal. But the experience of living with the Berbers in the village of Idirh up in the High Atlas left an indelible mark on all the team members.

Bryan finished his degree, then went on to complete a doctorate at Oxford. He subsequently got a job as a lecturer at the University of Edinburgh, and later became a professor of the new Department of Genetics at the University of Nottingham. He was also a fellow of the Royal Society, and was awarded the Linnaean Medal for Zoology, plus the Darwin-Wallace Medal from the Linnaean Society of London. Along with his wife Ann, he co-founded the Frozen Ark Project, with the aim of preserving DNA and living cells of endangered species worldwide. Bryan died in February 2014.

After Oxford, Colin Pennycuick completed a doctorate in

muscle physiology at Cambridge University, going on to work at Bristol University, the University of Miami and then back to Bristol. He also had a stint in Nairobi, Kenya in the late 1960s to study bat flight, plus two years as the deputy director of research at the Serengeti National Park. He became a leading authority on the flight of birds and bats and of bird navigation and migration, using Bristol University's first computer to design a wind tunnel which he then built from scratch. He also piloted a powered glider to study birds in flight. He was elected a fellow of the Royal Society and made an honorary companion of the Royal Aeronautical Society. Colin died in December 2019.

Charles Pasternak completed his doctorate in biochemistry at Oxford and went on to the Department of Pharmacology at Yale Medical School. He then returned to Oxford and set up the Department of Biochemistry, took up the Foundation Chair of Biochemistry at St George's Medical School in London and, on the weekends, was an Intelligence Officer in the Territorial Army, retiring with the rank of Major. In 1992, he founded the Oxford International Biomedical Centre, of which at the time of writing, he was still President.

For Humphrey Beckett, the experience of the university expedition to the High Atlas changed the entire course of his life. When I interviewed him, he looked back very fondly on his time in Morocco:

Humphrey: "I was one of those young Englishmen who always thought he would make his career outside England, somewhere in a colony or wherever it might be, and you might say the colonial service was an obvious possibility. But it was in Morocco up in the Atlas Mountains where we'd actually become useful providing medical care. I realised that, if I wished to make my life in the developing world, I needed to have a useful skill like medicine or engineering or be a teacher, so it was at that point I decided that I was doing the wrong subject, I should be doing medicine… so you see, my experience in the Atlas Mountains turned me from a historian, a possible colonial administrator (I'd have been hopeless at that), into a doctor, eventually ending up in psychiatry… All this negotiation between people actually helped to develop a capacity for empathy and seeing things from another person's point of view."

Having qualified as a medical doctor, Humphrey was shipped out to British Guiana where he was the sole medic for an area the size of Wales, with a population of 25,000 Amerindians. Returning to the UK, he trained in psychiatry and was soon shipped out again, this time as a lecturer in psychiatry at the University of Papua New Guinea. From there, it was off to New South Wales in Australia, then back to Britain working with prisoners with psychiatric disorders. He retired in 2000 and now lives in Australia.

Sadly, I discovered the other two members of the team died quite young. As far as I could find out, Peter Galloway completed his degree in Geography at Merton College but died not long after from tuberculosis. Botanist John Newbould went out to work at the Ngorongoro Crater conservation area in Tanzania. He was briefly mentioned in Anthony Smith's book *Throw out Two Hands* about a ballooning expedition across east Africa. As far as I could find out, John contracted some sort of disease and died in the mid-1960s.

Acknowledgements

This book would not have been possible without the generous input (by way of interviews, correspondence, provision of photos, diaries and other documents) from the members of the original 1955 'Oxford University Expedition to Southern Morocco': Prof Bryan Clarke, Dr Humphrey Beckett, Prof Colin Pennycuick and Dr Charles Pasternak. Each was very gracious in granting me permission to quote from various conversations and interviews, and from assorted notes and documents. Thanks also to Dr Ann Clarke for providing access to additional notes and photos from Prof Bryan Clarke's archive. I would also like to thank my nephew James Solomides for accompanying me (twice) as we ventured off into the unknown. Thanks also to Sharouk Mohammed Bin Saeed and Brahim Iherm Ben Nasser and their families, our generous hosts who welcomed us into their homes when we stayed in Idirh and Anammer. Final thanks to Chris Granlund, Dr Richard Rowe, Dr Ann Clarke, Dr Humphrey Beckett and Dr Charles Pasternak for providing feedback on the text of this book. Any errors are of course entirely down to the author.

Paul Olding is a BAFTA nominated, award-winning television Writer/Director and Producer. He has made over fifty films, traveling the globe to explore and document the natural world, ancient civilisations and the universe beyond. He has also written and directed a number of fictional short films and historical dramas. When Paul is not writing or making tv shows, he can be found on his vineyard in East Sussex.